"Dr. Walston has accomplished a phenomenal work on the topics of marriage, divorce, and remarriage. This book is biblically grounded and theologically sound. Walston is erudite, but he writes for the average layperson. He demonstrates that in a society with a high divorce rate there is still hope. The study questions that he provides at the end of each chapter are extremely beneficial for counselors, teachers, group studies, or personal study. This book is a must read for people in all walks of life who desire biblical knowledge on these topics."—Dr. Richard Riley, Senior Pastor of New Heights Wesleyan Church, Bloomington, IL

"I can honestly say that I have discovered more new nuggets of truth (with respect to both biblical information and interpretation) in Dr. Walston's book than in any other I have read on this difficult subject. Many such truths are subtle and some are huge, but all are helpful and practical. His additional points regarding the Old Testament bill of divorcement, research on the breadth of the word porneia, and thoughts on the one flesh relationship are just a few of the fresh elements in this book."—W. Berry Norwood, Senior Pastor First Southern Baptist Church, Scottsdale AZ

"Unmoved by denominational doctrine or tradition, Rick Walston takes a straight-ahead, Scripture-based look at an urgent subject gripping the church and America today."—Dr. Robert E. Gorrell, Senior Pastor of First United Methodist Church, Ardmore, OK

"This is the most biblically accurate book I have ever read on these topics. Writing from a serious and conservative reverence for biblical authority, Walston delves into many complex areas including adultery, fornication, spousal abuse, and clergy traditionalism. While Dr. Walston tackles all these issues with due academic care, his writing style is engaging and easy to comprehend. Furthermore, this book is set up as a study tool with excellent discussion questions after each chapter. This book should be required reading for all pastors and Christian counselors."—John Thornton, Pastor of Visitation and host of Radio Good News, Sioux Falls, SD

"I really enjoyed this book! It is probably one of the best, if not the best, examinations of the scriptures for the whole

marriage/divorce issue."—Len Bundy, youth pastor, Enumclaw, WA

"Rick Walston has taken us back to the clarity of Scripture, which in this case leads us to living in true Christian liberty, not license for selfish desire nor bondage to opinion. Walston rejects both certain "conservative" and "liberal" mores and points us to the final authority of Scripture: what does God say, not what does man think. This book is great treatment for a very difficult problem."—Tim Elliott, pastor and former chaplain

"Rick Walston's thorough reviews of how God regulated divorce and remarriage throughout scripture, and how these fit, or do not fit, present-day attitudes and situations is a refreshingly easy read. Ideal for counselors and pastors."—Dr. Douglas Batson, National Certified Counselor

"In a fragmented world, marriage and divorce are often viewed in merely secular ways. As a result, marriage has been devalued, divorce misunderstood, and God's will in these matters confused or even buried. Dr. Walston provides clear direction as he seeks to elucidate a biblical view of marriage and divorce. Steering clear of extremes, Dr. Walston carefully explores the relevant texts, deals with underlying theological issues, and takes into account the practical realities that affect human relationships in a fallen world. It is indeed rare to find a treatment of marriage and divorce that works through the issues in such an evenhanded, in-depth, yet accessible way."—Dr. Carmen C. DiCello, Senior Pastor

"In the difficult and confusing world of divorce and remarriage, it is always good to go back to the Bible and dig out anew the concepts and understandings of the biblical words. This is what Dr. Walston has done in this new book. Although some may disagree, due to preconceived concepts, with his conclusions, they have

been documented and expressed in terms of what they meant when they were inspired by the Holy Spirit and originally recorded in the Bible. This is a book worth careful study and careful research. It will allow one to see the depth and breath of what the Bible has to say on these issues."—Dr. Larry Allen, bi-vocational pastor/teacher

"Finally, truth and sense emerge from the fog of confusion and shame. Dr. Walston brings scriptural truth to a reality that many Christians live with today. This book is for those who struggle with the pain of divorce, for those who hope to be married again, and, especially, for those who struggle to extend grace to divorcés. Dr. Walston upholds the sanctity of marriage. While he does not arbitrarily condone divorce, he acknowledges that it occurs within the church, and he seeks to understand it. Through this book, many others will also understand these issues from a biblical perspective."—Marianne Stewart, Pastor of Women's Ministries, The Summit, Evangelical Free Church of America, Enumclaw, WA

"A painful subject treated with love and gentle humor by a masterful Bible teacher. Dr. Walston's wit, insight, and careful explanations capture the attention using real examples from his own pastoral experience. The scholarship and presentation engage without overwhelming. This book has a place in every pastor's study."—Roger Baker, Senior Pastor, First United Methodist Church, Brackettville, TX

"Rick Walston writes with the brilliance of a scholar, the warmhearted concern of a pastor, and the familiarity of a long-cherished friend. Read this book because you want to know the biblical position on the subject, but be forewarned: you will also be entertained, challenged, and educated in many other areas of thought."—Dr. David W. Bailey, Senior Pastor of Reformation Baptist Church, Tavares, FL

Something Happened On The Way To Happily Ever After

Something Happened On The Way To Happily Ever After

A Biblical View of Marriage, Divorce & Remarriage

by
Rick Walston

Wipf & Stock Publishers
Eugene, Oregon

Wipf & Stock Publishers
199 West 8th Avenue, Suite 3
Eugene, OR 97401

Something Happened On The Way To Happily Ever After: A Biblical View of Marriage, Divorce & Remarriage
ISBN: 1-59752-481-6

Dedicated to

My parents,
Lyle and Harriet Walston
*Through both good times and some of the most horrendous
times any parent should have to experience, they
demonstrated to their children what the vows
"till death do us part" really mean.*

~ and ~

My wife's parents,
Al and Colleen Insel
*Fifty-five years of marriage.
Role models of marriage wisdom.*

~ and ~

My wife,
Sue
My best friend. My committed companion.

Acknowledgments

Editing Helps and Comments:

During the writing of this book, one of my friends and one of my most helpful proofreaders Roberta Georgia Pendergrass (of Illinois) went to be with the Lord. Roberta was a graduate student earning her master's degree in apologetics. She spent many hours reading this manuscript and making exceptionally helpful and insightful suggestions.

Others with helpful suggestions and insights were Larry Allen, Roger Baker, David Bailey, Carmen DiCello, W. Berry Norwood, Eric Odell-Hein, Holly Osborne, Tyler Ramey, Richard Riley, and Sue Walston.

Book Cover:

The cover of this book is a picture that I took at Cannon Beach, Oregon, of Haystack Rock. The title of the picture is "Lone Shadow" © 2006.

Encouragement and Support:

As always, I wish to thank the love of my life, my wife, Sue, for her *constant encouragement* and *unflinching support*. She is truly a gift from the Lord.

I also wish to thank the many students and friends who kept after me, *hounding me*, to put into writing my many years of study, teaching, and counseling on these topics.

Table of Contents

Chapter 3

Chapter 4

Chapter 12

Chapter 13

Foreword

John, in the first chapter of his Gospel, declared Jesus to be, "full of grace and truth" (John 1:14). I find Rick Walston's book on this important subject of a biblical view of divorce and remarriage to be just that—full of *grace* and *truth*.

Rick is an educator, author, and speaker. He is also a man of innovation and creativity. However, in this book, more than anything else, it is the heart of a shepherd-teacher that comes through. Rick shares from a place of deep concern for those "bowed" and "broken" by the heart-rending effects of divorce, to see them receive the help and healing they need to move forward in their lives in Christ, finding a biblical pathway towards remarriage or reconciliation. At the same time, he writes from a place of intense passion to see Christian marriages contended for by the power of the Word and the Spirit, so that divorce never becomes an option.

As a pastoral leader, and as one who has walked with countless couples and individuals through miraculous reconciliations, emotional devastations, and most everything in between, I find this book to be beyond helpful. It deals with this subject with clarity, courage, and conviction. Rick is never strident, self-righteous, or condescending, but at the same time, he maintains an unflinching commitment to let the Scriptures guide us through this demanding subject and its attendant difficulties. He accomplishes this with deep compassion, sound biblical reasoning, and when appropriate, healthy doses of good humor.

I believe this book comes "not a moment too soon." The divorce rate of Evangelical Christians is a national tragedy and travesty. And while I have a deep love for all affected by the pain of divorce, I, nonetheless, see a need for a clarion, prophetic call for marital covenant keeping to be sounded, calling us back to our ultimate Covenant Keeper, God Himself. In this book, Rick does just that, and I thank him for it.

I like the way Rick thinks—sanely and soundly. I like the way Rick works—thoroughly and thoughtfully. I like the way Rick writes—clearly and creatively.

I like *Something Happened On The Way To Happily Ever After*, and I believe you'll like it too.

Dale Evrist, Senior Pastor
New Song Christian Fellowship
Brentwood, Tennessee

Something Happened On The Way To
"Happily Ever After"
A Biblical View of Marriage, Divorce & Remarriage

Introductory Remarks

Why yet another book on the topics of marriage, divorce, and remarriage? Anyone who has done even a little research knows that there are plenty of books out there on these topics.

However, I felt a need to write this present book due to the fact that while there are many books out there, they seem too often to be pushing an agenda. Some books are written from a certain denominational stance.[1]

Others are written to justify something that has transpired in the author's life.[2]

There are, to be sure, some authors who have written on these topics who attempt to simply stay true to the Word of God and reflect what God has truly said about these issues.

---

[1] I myself wrote such a book for the Assemblies of God. Rick L. Walston, *Divorce and remarriage: An amplification of the Assemblies of God position paper on divorce and remarriage* (Gospel Publishing House, 1991).

[2] Amazingly, some Christians change their theology to fit events in their lives. A pastor I know used to believe that as long as there was no adultery involved, a Christian couple had no scriptural grounds for divorce. But, when his daughter was unhappy with her new husband, his theology changed, and he then believed that divorce between Christians was OK if they simply were not happy with each other.

However, most of these are academic books written at a level that is not easy reading. The average Christian does not read academic books.

I have attempted to bridge the gap with this book. It is written for those struggling to make heads or tails about the dilemmas faced because of divorce. It is written for both those with firsthand experience of this issue and for those attempting to minister to people who have faced or who are facing divorce.

As both a former pastor and present-day academic, I am generally torn about the level at which I should write articles and books. Sometimes when my materials are too scholarly, people have responded by saying that they wish I'd tone down my work so that they could more easily understand it. One woman complained that, "You PhD's could make opening a can of soup difficult." However, with this present work, I had no such internal debate.

For The Normal Christian

With all of that in mind, this book is for the normal, everyday Christian. I wrote this book for those who have not spent a day in seminary and who don't know the difference between a transliteration and a translation, and they won't need to.

That, however, does not mean that I have "dumbed-down" the information herein. I give Christian readers more credit than to patronize them with oversimplified argumentations. Some people today are saying that Christians don't read anymore. Apparently, all information must be transmitted on the "big screen." I do not believe this is entirely true. Christianity is, after all, the religion of a book, the Holy Scriptures. I think that most Christians like to read. Perhaps what makes some Christians today not want to read is more simple than some societal, postmodern shift. Maybe it's just that some of the books and articles out there are not worth reading. Let me quickly state that I am not implying that my writing is stupendous or that this book will be a "page turner." However, I have honestly attempted to make this book enjoyable, lay-level reading, given both the difficult and delicate topics it deals with.

This book is my attempt to put into plain language what I believe God says in his Holy Word about the topics of marriage, divorce, and remarriage.

Obviously this book is neither exhaustive nor definitive. It was not meant to be. I believe it does, however, clearly and truly represent a solidly biblical view on these issues.

I will leave it to my readers to determine if I have succeeded in my goal.

Confession

Above I stated that many books push an agenda. Some push a particular denominational perspective and others attempt to justify something that has transpired in the author's life.

My personal journey into this topic is opposite from many. In my early years as a Christian, I was taught that there should never be divorce and remarriage for any reason. Then, as a graduate student, I set out to write a thesis which would substantiate my preconceived beliefs. I was astounded by what I discovered.

Serious biblical research led me to evidence that showed that what I believed was wrong. As a Christian, I am always excited to find evidence that leads me into God's truth, even if it means that I have to change my former beliefs.

I am a theologian. When I find evidence that what I believe is wrong, I am just as excited as when I find evidence that what I believe is right. God's truth, not our preconceived ideas or beliefs, should always be our goal.

I would ask that the reader attempt to hold at bay his or her preconceived ideas and beliefs on these topics long enough to allow the biblical evidence to speak for itself.

We should always be prepared to accept God's truth wherever it leads us.

*"You do not regulate something you forbid
You just forbid it. Once it is forbidden,
it is utterly off limits." —Rick Walston*

Chapter 1

God Regulates Divorce and Remarriage

I was just voted in as the senior pastor of a small church in Longview, Washington, in the Pacific Northwest. I had already worked as the associate pastor at this same church for a few years. Now, of course, I was excited to be the lead pastor, and I threw myself into this new position with great gusto.

There was an older couple named Don and Aubrey[3] in the church who came from the "old school" as they called it. By "old school" they meant several things. They were suspicious of anything that they perceived as new; they didn't like the new worship songs that my music minister and I brought to the church; they didn't understand why sermons had to be "tape recorded"; they didn't like the use of any other Bible in church services but the *King James Version*, and they certainly were not keen on this young, upstart preacher.

It's Just Wrong

When the topic of divorce and remarriage came up in the church, they were quite vocal about their opinions. Their position was, "It's just wrong." No amount of explanations about certain situations that Moses, Paul, or even Jesus

---

[3] To protect people, all the names of people and churches are fictitious but the stories are real, though some of them are amalgamations.

addressed helped them see that there had to be more to a biblical view of divorce and remarriage than simply, "It's just wrong."

Once the subject of divorce and remarriage had come up, Don and Aubrey seemed to steer nearly every conversation back to this subject so they could voice their opinions about it. One Sunday after church, a few of us went to lunch. People were talking about everything from the food they had ordered to the Seattle Seahawks' chances (or lack thereof) to have a good season that year. But, true to their hobbyhorse, Don and Aubrey brought up the topics of divorce and remarriage, and then they proceeded to explain to the people at their end of the table how, *"Pastor Rick is young and doesn't know what he's talking about. Divorce and remarriage are simply wrong, all the time, and people shouldn't do it, period."*

Divorce, Candy, and Rat Poison

I listened to them for awhile as they insisted that divorce and remarriage should simply never happen and when it does, it is always sin. Then I asked them a few questions:

> "Don and Aubrey, I have a few questions for you," I said.

> "Okay, shoot," said Don.

> "You have two grown children, right?" I asked.

> "Yes," said Aubrey. "Two boys."

> "Well, tell me. Did you ever allow your boys to eat rat poison?" I asked.

> "What!?" Aubrey was shocked.

> "Rat poison," I repeated. "Did you ever allow your kids to eat rat poison?"

They were visibly upset at my odd question. Don became defensive and spoke up:

"Of course not! What kind of a stupid question is that?" he demanded.

I went on:

"Well, did you ever allow your kids to eat candy?"

They both hesitated, and then Aubrey said:

"Well, yes, of course, occasionally."

"Did you allow your kids to eat candy right before dinnertime?" I asked.

"No," Aubrey said, still defensive.

"Why not?" I asked.

"I didn't want them to ruin their appetite before dinner," she answered.

"Well, if it wasn't near dinnertime, did you allow them to go ahead and eat all of the candy they wanted?" I asked.

"No!" Aubrey said. "I allowed them to eat a little, only in reasonable amounts."

"So, why didn't you allow your kids to eat rat poison in little, reasonable amounts?" I asked.

"Because that would be stupid and it could kill them. There are no little, reasonable amounts of rat poison that you can feed a child," Don answered, still angry.

> "So, let me get this straight," I said, "you regulated how much candy your kids could eat, but you did not regulate how much rat poison they could eat; you just forbade the rat poison altogether?"

They thought for a moment and then Don answered:

> "That's right. We regulated the amount of candy they could have, but we would never even consider allowing them to eat even an ounce of rat poison. Candy is OK in some cases, but rat poison never is."

To this I said:

> "You do not regulate something you forbid. You just forbid it. Once it is forbidden, it is utterly off limits."

Don agreed and said:

> "Right. It's forbidden, so it's out of the question."

Then I said:

> "So if divorce and remarriage are simply forbidden as you say it is, why do you suppose God regulates them throughout the Bible?"

Neither wanted to answer my question because the "trap had been sprung" on them. So, I answered it for them: *"Because, He does not simply forbid divorce and remarriage,"* I said.

Moses Regulated Divorce and Remarriage

 Though we will deal with these passages more in depth later, we shall now investigate some Scriptures that show that God does not forbid divorce; rather, He *regulates* it.

> If a man marries a woman who becomes displeasing to him because he finds something indecent about her, and *he writes her a certificate of divorce*, gives it to her and *sends her from his house*, and if after she leaves his house *she becomes the wife of another man* (remarriage), and her second husband dislikes her and *writes her a certificate of divorce*, gives it to her and *sends her from his house*, or if he dies, then her first husband, who divorced her, is not allowed to marry her again after she has been defiled. That would be detestable in the eyes of the LORD. Do not bring sin upon the land the LORD your God is giving you as an inheritance (emphasis mine, Deuteronomy 24:1-4).[4]

Given the impassioned rhetoric about this topic by many Christians today, this passage is striking in its noticeable lack of emotion. This passage talks about divorce and remarriage in a nonchalant and disimpassioned tone. Neither divorce nor remarriage is forbidden in this passage. The only thing that is forbidden in this passage is a remarriage between the wife and her first husband after she has been married to a second man who either divorces her or who dies.

It is important, however, to make clear that the Bible does not encourage divorce. Likewise, this specific passage does not encourage it. But, it does clearly regulate it.

Jesus Regulated Divorce and Remarriage

> Some Pharisees came to him to test him. They asked, "Is it lawful for a man to *divorce his wife for any and every reason*?" "Haven't you read," he replied, "that at the beginning the Creator 'made them male and female,' and said, 'For this reason a man will leave his father and mother and be united to his wife, and the two

---

[4] All Scripture references are from the *New International Version* unless otherwise noted.

> will become one flesh'? So they are no longer two, but one. Therefore what God has joined together, let man not separate." "Why then," they asked, "did Moses *command* that a man give his wife a certificate of divorce and send her away?" Jesus replied, "Moses *permitted* you to divorce your wives because your hearts were hard. But it was not this way from the beginning. I tell you that anyone who divorces his wife, *except for marital unfaithfulness*, and marries another woman commits adultery" (emphasis mine, Matthew 19:3-9).

In this very telling passage, Jesus clears up some confused thinking that was common in His day. The Pharisees, and even His own disciples, were under the mistaken impression that Moses—and thus by extension God Himself—had *commanded* men to divorce their wives under certain conditions. To their confused minds, it was a "religious duty" to divorce their wives under certain circumstances. Jesus clears up this confusion and says that Moses never *commanded* divorce; he only *permitted* it. Why had he permitted it? Because of the hardness of men's hearts. So, while God does not want people to divorce nor does He command them to do so, He does *allow* divorce under certain conditions. Jesus Himself regulates divorce and remarriage in this passage when he says, "except for marital unfaithfulness." In other words He says that divorce and remarriage are permissible—not commanded—when there has been "marital unfaithfulness," i.e., adultery.

Paul Regulated Divorce and Remarriage

> To the married I give this command (not I, but the Lord): A wife must not separate from her husband. But if she does, she must remain unmarried or else be reconciled to her husband. And a husband must not divorce his wife. To the rest I say this (I, not the Lord):

If any brother has a wife who is not a believer and she is willing to live with him, he must not divorce her. And if a woman has a husband who is not a believer and he is willing to live with her, she must not divorce him. For the unbelieving husband has been sanctified through his wife, and the unbelieving wife has been sanctified through her believing husband. Otherwise your children would be unclean, but as it is, they are holy. But if the unbeliever leaves, let him do so. A believing man or woman is not bound in such circumstances; God has called us to live in peace (1 Corinthians 7:10-15).

Paul's words are so clear here that they hardly need a commentary of explanation. However, because this passage has been abused by some interpreters, we shall review the facts herein.

In verses 10 and 11 the context is set, and it is clearly about divorce. Paul says that "A wife must not separate from her husband. But if she does, she must remain unmarried" (v. 11)—*unmarried* in this context is clearly "divorced." It is simple logic that a woman cannot be married to a man and unmarried at the same time. So, if Paul says that she is to remain "unmarried," it is simply another way of saying that she is "divorced" and she is to remain single.

Then, Paul states in verses 12 and 13 that if a Christian is married to a non-Christian and the non-Christian does not want a divorce, the believer must not divorce him or her.

However, in verse 15, Paul goes on to say that if the non-Christian spouse wishes to leave (the context is divorce), the Christian spouse is to allow the person to do so. In such circumstances, the Christian is not "bound" to the marriage.

Misunderstanding Paul

Not all agree with my comments about Paul's words in this passage. Some have attempted to say that Paul does not allow for divorce in verse 15.

Note that Paul does not use the word "divorce" in verse 15. He says rather, "But if the unbeliever leaves, *let him do so*." Some suggest that something less than divorce is meant here. Two quick points need to be made.

First, arguably the most basic rule of interpretation is investigating verses in their context. The context of this passage is clearly about the issue of divorce. Paul was addressing this issue because the Corinthian Christians had asked him specifically about divorce. Thus, it is clear from the context that when Paul says that "if the unbeliever leaves, *let him do so*," he is talking about divorce.

Second, if we were to concede that Paul was not talking about divorce in verse 15 — and we do not — it would not erase the fact that Moses and Jesus do regulate divorce.

One author attempted to convince his readers that Paul was not allowing for actual divorce. When he finished his argument, he concluded with these words: "Therefore, God does not allow for divorce."

The obvious problem with his conclusion is threefold: (1) His conclusion was based upon only one passage; (2) His interpretation of that one passage was highly questionable; (3) Most importantly, however, was the fact that his conclusion flatly contradicted the teachings of Moses and Jesus on this topic.

The author's conclusion would have been less objectionable had he stated: "Therefore, in this particular situation Paul does not allow for divorce." I think that this would still be an erroneous conclusion; nonetheless, it would have been better for the author to ascribe the lack of allowance for divorce only to Paul's teaching within this very narrow context.

Another principle of biblical interpretation is that we cannot accept one passage to the exclusion of another. Even if Paul had never given any allowance for divorce and remarriage, this would not undo the prior teachings of both Moses and Jesus. It would mean only that Paul did not address the same conditions under which Moses and Jesus allowed for divorce and remarriage.

Conclusion: God Regulates Divorce and Remarriage

Though we have only reviewed in a cursory fashion three passages (Deuteronomy 24:1-4; Matthew 19:3-9; 1 Corinthians 7:10-15), it is obvious that God does not simply *forbid* divorce and remarriage.

Just as parents do not forbid their children from eating candy, but they regulate it, so too God has not forbidden divorce and remarriage; rather, He regulates them.

Throughout the remainder of this book, we shall look more closely at these passages and many others, and we will discuss the details of God's regulations of divorce and remarriage.

Study Questions For

Chapter 1
God Regulates Divorce and Remarriage

1. What is the author's point when he says, "You do not regulate something that you forbid. You just forbid it. Once it is forbidden, it is utterly off limits."
2. Did Moses regulate divorce and remarriage? Give Scripture.
3. Did Jesus regulate divorce and remarriage? Give Scripture.
4. Did Paul regulate divorce and remarriage? Give Scripture.
5. What parallel to divorce and remarriage is the author making when he talks about the fact that parents do not forbid their children from eating candy, but they regulate it?

The difficulty with marriage is that we fall in love with a personality, but must live with a character.—Peter de Vries

Chapter 2

The Divorced and Remarried

"Hello?" The phone conversation started like any other.

"Pastor Walston?" She asked.

"Yes. This is he," I responded.

"You don't know me but my name is Anna Curell. I attend Life Center Church here in town, and I was wondering if I can talk with you."

"Sure" I said, "what can I do for you?"

"Do you know my pastor, Victor Marks?" she asked.

I did know her pastor. Two pastors ministering in the same small community for more than a decade have opportunities to meet occasionally. We were not close, but I had spent a little ministry time with him talking about our community. He seemed like a nice enough guy, with a large successful ministry. His church was one of the largest in our small northwest town. Funny, isn't it, how we often determine "success" by sheer size. I knew nearly nothing of his theology, other than he pastored a Christian church which was affiliated with a respectable Christian denomination.

"Yes, I know your pastor," I responded.

At that moment, the woman on the phone began to sob. She told me that even though her pastor had encouraged her to divorce her adulterous and physically abusive husband years earlier, he would not now perform her new wedding to a wonderful Christian man who attended their church.

"Wait. I'm not following you here. Let me understand. Pastor Marks encouraged you to divorce your first husband because he was an adulterer and physically abusive?" I asked.

"Yes," she said. "My husband used to beat me on a fairly regular basis. He'd get drunk, or just plain angry, and beat me. I lived with it for years until my doctors and finally Pastor Marks realized that my husband was really going to hurt me. Not only that, but my husband also had a habit of committing adultery."

"So, how long ago did you divorce your husband?"

"About seven years," she said.

"And, now you have met a Christian man who attends your church, and you want to marry him but your pastor will not perform the wedding?"

"That's right," she said.

"Who is your fiancé?" I asked.

"His name is Gerald and he's wonderful. His first wife died of cancer about ten years ago. He moved here from California five years ago," she said.

"So, what does Pastor Marks think of Gerald?" I asked.

"Oh, he likes him a lot. They go golfing together all the time," she said.

"Well, then, exactly why won't your pastor marry the two of you?" I asked.

"Because I'm divorced," she said.

Puzzled, I said, "But, you just said that Pastor Marks was *the one* who encouraged you to divorce your first husband."

"Yes. But he says that he won't do a wedding ceremony for people who are divorced," she said, still crying.

Even More Disturbing

As if that whole scenario wasn't disturbing enough, it became even worse as Anna continued. Anna's pastor had told her to find another pastor outside of "his church" to marry them. That's why she had called me.

To add insult to injury, Anna had a terminal disease, and she would not be around much longer to enjoy life with her new husband. All she wanted was to spend the little time she had left "as the wife of this wonderful Christian man," as she put it.

Keep Paying Your Tithes

Pastor Marks told this couple that after another pastor in the community had performed their wedding ceremony, these newlyweds were to attend his church and pay their tithes to his church. What was even more amazing than all of this was the fact that this couple was so bamboozled by this pastor, that they had full intentions of getting married in another church (one that would accept them) and then return to Pastor Marks' church!

Don't Let Them Treat You that Way

Why do divorced and remarried people allow themselves to be abused by others, including pastors like Anna's? What self-respecting person would ever return to the church and pastor described above? And, what is it about some pastors that makes them believe that divorced people aren't good enough to be a part of their "family," but their money is good enough to receive?

I think that for those who've been abused there are a couple of reasons. First, many people get their eyes off Christ and become mesmerized by their pastors. This is sometimes so acute that people tend to believe every word a pastor says as though he can do or say no wrong. Second, they are often ignorant of the most basic elements of the gospel of Christ, like, for instance, forgiveness. Oh, people talk about God's forgiveness, but some have a difficult time really believing or understanding that God has fully forgiven them.

As for some pastors (and some others in leadership), they likewise have a couple of "reasons" for abusing the divorced and remarried. First, some pastors—believe it or not—are just as ignorant about what the Bible says about this topic as many laypeople are. They often *sound* informed as they quote Scripture and loudly trumpet their opinions from the pulpit, but many times they are only repeating what they have been told by their denominational leaders, who were repeating what their leaders had told them, and so on. Second, it is hard to go against the current. Many pastors repeat what they're taught because they want to have the praise and acceptance of their peers. Any alert pastor who has attended a pastors' conference has seen this to be true. Their fear of being an outcast makes some of them "keep the faith," even if "the faith" they are keeping may be nothing more than denominational traditionalism.

Love the Sinner

Before we move more fully into a biblical discussion about the topics of divorce and remarriage, it is important to talk about the divorced and remarried. One thing that we must keep in mind is that neither divorce nor remarriage is an abstract concept that has no bearing on real-life individuals. Of course we are not to derive our theology based upon how people feel. But it is important to see this topic in relation to real life, and that means that we must respectfully consider the *people* of divorce and remarriage.

Too often leaders and others in the Christian church have treated the divorced and remarried as second-class citizens in the kingdom of God. The story of Anna is just one real-life example of this sort of mistreatment.

It's interesting that Revelation 21:8 says, "But the cowardly, the unbelieving, the vile, the murderers, the sexually immoral, those who practice magic arts, the idolaters and all liars—their place will be in the fiery lake of burning sulfur. This is the second death." In our Christian redemption theology, all those listed in this verse can find forgiveness for their sins and Christian acceptance if they repent. In fact, there have been converts whose sinful practices, such as murder and witchcraft, were extolled in certain Christian circles as indicating to what extent God will forgive sins. One of my evangelist friends says that "God saves from the guttermost to the uttermost." I remember a time when Christian speakers who drew the largest crowds in evangelistic services were those who had committed the worst crimes. If a former gang member who had committed murders and the most vile sins imaginable was the keynote speaker, the place would be packed. Interestingly, many of these types of evangelistic services were little more than a recounting of the person's sinful lifestyle. After nearly an hour of recounting the horrendous sins that the speaker had committed, the story of his conversion to Christ was neatly tacked on to the last five to ten minutes of the service. I spoke with people who had been Christians nearly their entire lives who lamented that they did not have an "outstanding testimony."

It seemed that for a season, Christians *en masse* ran to and fro to listen to these extreme converts and extend the "right hand of fellowship" and acceptance to them. However, many of these same accepting people held the divorced and remarried at bay with an attitude that was less than accepting. While former murderers, drug addicts, prostitutes, and sorcerers were embraced with Christian charity, the divorced and remarried often found themselves left out of the charitable circle of acceptance.

God is a Divorcé

It comes as a shock to many to learn that God himself is a divorcé. God says in Jeremiah 3:8a, "*I gave* faithless Israel her *certificate of divorce and sent her away* because of all her adulteries" (emphasis mine). In the context of this passage, Israel had committed adultery, and God divorced her.

In an interesting e-mail conversation with a man who had written to me about God being divorced, he wrote: "You are wrong! The Bible teaches over and over again that God is married to the backslider, and that He is faithful even to the adulterous generation, and that He wants the same from his people!"

So, I asked him if he'd ever read Jeremiah. Certainly there was forgiveness and reconciliation for backslidden Israel; however, she had to repent. God says:

> Go, proclaim this message toward the north: "Return, faithless Israel," declares the LORD, "I will frown on you no longer, for I am merciful," declares the LORD, "I will not be angry forever. Only acknowledge your guilt—you have rebelled against the LORD your God, you have scattered your favors to foreign gods under every spreading tree, and have not obeyed me," declares the LORD (Jeremiah 3: 12-13).

To deny that God is a divorcé is to deny the Scriptures. Another passage that talks about God's divorce is Isaiah 50:1, "This is what the LORD says: '*Where is your mother's certificate of divorce with which I sent her away*? Or to which of my creditors did I sell you? Because of your sins you were sold; because of your transgressions your mother *was sent away*'" (emphasis mine).

There have been some who have attempted to lessen the impact of the concept of God being a divorcé by saying that, first, God was only using anthropomorphic language, i.e., human terminology, to make His point, and, second, God did this only to get Israel to repent. Therefore, God was not truly a divorced person.

Even if these two points were true, it is astonishing that God would show Himself as the initiator of a divorce. James 1:13b says, "For God cannot be tempted by evil, nor does he tempt anyone." If divorce is the evil that many people say it is, then it is all the more astounding that God would voluntarily place Himself in that picture! It is simply unthinkable that God would picture Himself as a sinner to make a point.

Concerning their second point, that God divorced Israel only to get Israel to repent: since when does the end justify the means? Remember, God cannot sin or tempt others to sin (James 1:13b). If divorce is the sin that many make it out to be, then God used sin to get sinners to repent. This is a convoluted absurdity.

A Justified Divorce

Of course, we know that God is without sin. Thus, His divorce from Israel was not sin. God was justified to divorce Israel, and many people are justified to divorce their adulterous spouses as we shall see later.

However, the issue, at least for this chapter, is simply this: how are we to treat the divorced and remarried person? How should we treat God? He is a divorcé. We should not gloss over the fact that God did divorce Israel, nor should we gloss over the fact that God forgives all sinners who repent, even the divorced and remarried.

Study Questions For

Chapter 2
The Divorced and Remarried

1. What might be some reasons why divorced and remarried people allow themselves to be abused by others?
2. What are a couple of "reasons" that the author gives that some pastors (and others in leadership) abuse the divorced and remarried?
3. Is God is a divorcé? Give Scripture.
4. To deny that God is a divorcé is to deny what?
5. What does the author call "a convoluted absurdity"?

Almost no one is foolish enough to imagine that he automatically deserves great success in any field of activity; yet almost everyone believes that he automatically deserves success in marriage. — Sydney J. Harris

Chapter 3

What is Marriage?

The Bitter Woman

In the mid-1980's, Virginia Blake was a 60-year-old woman whose husband, Fred, had divorced her 30 years earlier. Virginia and Fred were Christians. However, when Fred divorced her, Virginia had serious doubts about her ex-husband's salvation. After all, Virginia's church taught that there was no biblical reason for divorce or remarriage. According to them, all divorce and remarriage was sin. Since Fred had divorced Virginia, it was a sure sign to Virginia and her fellow church members that Fred was not a *real* Christian.

According to Virginia's church, the only reason a person could remarry is if his or her spouse had died. So, even though Virginia's ex-husband, Fred, was remarried and had children by his second wife, she remained single.

Over the years, many saw Virginia as "a martyr for truth." People would talk about her in low tones and voice their sorrow for her: "She lives all alone," they'd say almost mournfully. "She's so very holy" some would suggest. Most of her fellow church members revered her as a pious woman who opted to remain single instead of committing the "sin of remarriage."

However, this "pious" woman had grown austere, bitter, and mean-spirited. Contrary to Jesus' teachings on forgiving those who offend you, she had never learned the virtue of forgiveness. And contrary to the warning given by the writer of Hebrews, "See to it that no one misses the grace of God and that no bitter root grows up to cause trouble and defile many" (12:15), her anger and unforgiveness had turned to a poisonous bitterness that infected many who got close to her. She was curt and insensitive to nearly everyone she talked to.

Her clothing style had seemingly frozen in time. Her dowdy appearance made her look a decade older than she was. She wore very little make up (if any) and her hair generally looked as though she had her own time machine which she would use to travel back about 25 years to have it coifed (styled).

The church's general reverence for Virginia notwithstanding, not everyone was impressed with this local "martyr." Some daring souls suggested that she purposely took on this beleaguered appearance because it magnified her "martyr" persona. Some suggested that her unforgiveness had caused her to stop growing socially many years before. Virginia was always quick to let others know that she "lived alone and was suffering for Jesus and His Word." Not only did she appear as the sorrowful woman, but she made a point of infecting younger women in the church with her ideas.

Kimberly was 34 years old and had never been married in spite of her stunning good looks and charming personality. She had grown up in the church, and she had prayed all her life that God would direct her to a husband who would share her strong Christian faith. When she met Mike, she felt that God had brought them together. Mike was also 34, and he was a minister in a different church, but it was the same denomination of which Kimberly and Virginia were members. The only problem was that Mike had been divorced. Mike's wife, Linda, had left him for another man. Though Mike had worked very hard at holding his marriage together, even to the point of forgiving Linda and begging her to leave the "other man" and return home, she simply would not repent. Then, she began living with her new boyfriend. Since he was not a Christian, Linda stopped going to church. Then she filed the legal papers and secured a divorce from Mike. Later she married her boyfriend.

With a 100 percent confidence vote by his church, Mike continued to lead the church as their senior pastor. All of the members of the church knew the events of Mike's divorce and they unanimously agreed that while he was not perfect, he had done all he could to save the marriage and that his first wife simply had gone her own way into sin.

For the next four years Mike continued to pastor the church. Then, he met, dated, and became engaged to Kimberly. Everyone at Mike's church was thrilled. Kimberly was a wonderful Christian woman and Mike's church members were nearly as excited about the marriage as he and Kimberly were.

But, as soon as Virginia learned that Kimberly was engaged to a formerly married man, she went out of her way to confront Kimberly. Virginia told her that as long as the minister's ex-wife was alive, then Kimberly could not marry him. In fact, Virginia took it a step further and told Kimberly that it would be better for her never to marry. Kimberly should be like Virginia and stay single. After all, Virginia was about Kimberly's age when her husband had left her. It did not matter to Virginia that the minister's wife had committed adultery nor that she was now remarried. Virginia simply told Kimberly that it was "wrong" and a "sin" for her to marry the divorced minister.

Kimberly weighed Virginia's words against the Scripture. According to Kimberly's understanding of the pertinent Scriptures on this topic, she decided that it was not wrong to marry Mike. During my last communication with them, I found that Kimberly and Mike are still happily married (almost deliriously so) after 17 years, and together they are serving the Lord in ministry.

The Three Marriage Models

In various human societies, marriage has often been seen in one of three models. However, in the Judeo-Christian perspective, marriage is an institution created and sanctified by God. Let's review the three models.

Marriage Model # 1: An Invention of Necessity

Marriage as an invention of necessity is an atheistic idea of marriage. It is a base, animalistic idea of marriage that comes primarily from the evolutionary concept of human ancestry. In essence, this model says that man, as an evolving animal, needed to propagate the species. He did so by attaching himself to a woman for the purpose of reproduction, as well as for his base physical desires and drives, which are also part of the evolutionary trigger to sustain the species. Not only would he need to have a physical relationship with the woman, he would also need to protect his offspring from others who would do them harm. This protection is better done by two parents than by one. So, man *invented marriage out of necessity* as a way not only to reproduce but to sustain his offspring so that the species in general and his genes in particular would continue on.

Certainly, even in this atheistic model, there would also be a base physical attraction. So, there is this primary twofold idea of marriage that derives from the evolutionary model: propagation of the species and attraction. However, this model is centered upon the humans' need for propagation and self-satisfaction. Furthermore, if either partner in this marriage wants to propagate children with someone else, or if he or she simply finds someone else more desirable, he or she may simply move on with the new partner. Thus, *life-long commitment* was never a key element in this model.

This model really says nothing of the concept of marriage itself. That men and women marry for the purpose of propagation does not lift the concept of marriage any further than simply an invention of necessity.

Marriage Model # 2: A Convention of Society

Marriage as a convention of society is a legal idea of marriage. Taking marriage a step further than simply an invention of necessity, this second model elevates the concept of marriage above the first model. In this second model, marriage is seen as a contract between two people who agree to be legally bound to each other by societal laws. In this model the concept of marriage itself begins to have some intrinsic value. A marriage contract is binding upon the two people who agree to it.

Consequence Clauses

However, as the old saying goes, contracts are made to be broken. By their very nature, contracts have "consequence clauses" which state what will happen if one or both parties break the contract. The very fact that "consequence clauses" are built into the contract shows that it is intrinsically breakable.

Either party (or both) can break a contract by simply getting a divorce for any reason. The fact that there is a contract simply means that there will be some consequences when there is a divorce, not unlike any normal contract between two parties.

If I hire someone to paint my house, and we sign a contract to that effect, and then he paints only half of my house and stops, he has broken the contract. The consequences will be that I will not pay him what I have "contracted" to pay him. So, while contracts have a certain amount of legal weight to them, they are really nothing more than a written agreement that the two parties will do what they promise to do. And, if one person breaks the contract, then the other party to the contract is entitled to compensation in the form of the contractually established consequences. In this second model of marriage, divorce is an ever-present option with some legal consequences. Thus, *life-long commitment* is not a key element in the convention-of-society model, in spite of the fact that many who believe in this second model of marriage have the words "till death do us part" in their marriage vows.

Marriage Model # 3: A Covenant of Marriage

Marriage as a covenant is the biblical model of marriage. A covenant is a superior contract. It is not simply a contract between two people; it is, rather, a covenant between the two marriage partners and a Third Person, God. In the covenant of marriage, God actually joins the marriage partners together and makes them one.

> So the LORD God caused the man to fall into a deep sleep; and while he was sleeping, he took one of the man's ribs and closed up the place with flesh. Then the LORD God made a woman from the rib he had taken out of the man, and he brought her to the man. The man said, "This is now bone of my bones and flesh of my flesh; she shall be called 'woman,' for she was taken out of man." For this reason a man will leave his father and mother and be united to his wife, and they will become one flesh (Genesis 2:21-24).

Since this is the case, it is not a man-made institution that can be simply disregarded as though it were nothing more than an ordinary contract between two people. Referring to Genesis 2:21-24, Jesus says:

> "Haven't you read," he replied, "that at the beginning the Creator 'made them male and female,' and said, 'For this reason a man will leave his father and mother and be united to his wife, and the two will become one flesh'? So they are no longer two, but one. Therefore what God has joined together, let man not separate" (Matthew 19:4-6).

This is no mere invention of necessity or convention of society. Our Lord says this is the blending of two lives into "one flesh."

By Death Alone

Note also that according to the covenant, there are no "consequence clauses" in case one or both of the parties break the covenant. Thus, according to the Bible, when two people get married, they are promising before God and their human witnesses that they shall be united in marriage until death separates them. In this third, biblical concept, marriage itself is intrinsically valuable. It is not just an invention of necessity, nor is it merely a convention of society. It is not simply "a legal contract" that can be broken with little or no consequences. It is, rather, a covenant designed by God. To break it is to sin not only against the spouse but also against the Third Person of the covenant, God Himself.

In the first two models, a spouse might commit adultery, and if so, the idea is that the only person offended is the other spouse. However, in the *covenant* of marriage, a spouse not only sins against his or her partner by committing adultery, but the person actually sins against God Himself.

Capital Punishment

In the Old Testament, when a spouse committed adultery, he or she was put to death by stoning. "If a man commits adultery with another man's wife—with the wife of his neighbor—both the adulterer and the adulteress must be put to death" (Leviticus 20:10). In God's original design, death was to be the only thing that broke the marriage covenant, and if one committed adultery, that one was put to death. Thus, the consequence of breaking the covenant of marriage (by adultery) was death (this will be discussed more later.)

Not Optional

These three models are not options from which people may select when they get married. In other words, a couple cannot say, "That *covenant model* is too binding, so we'll just take model number two." These are not options; these are the three basic models that people have *believed*. If the third model is the correct one—which is what this author believes—then all people in all marriages for all time are under model number three whether they know it or not. Since God is the author of marriage, then He is the Third Person of the covenant in all marriages of all people.

So, all marriages of all people are covenants between the marriage partners and God. Since God is the *creator and designer* of the marriage union, it is up to Him to set the rules of marriage, and we who enter into a marriage union must accept His terms and rules.

The Biblical Concept of Marriage

Marriage originated in the mind of God. It is not a human invention nor is it a human convention. Marriage is a God-ordained, human-divine relationship. The Scripture makes this clear.

> So God created man in his own image, in the image of God he created him; male and female he created them. God blessed them and said to them, "Be fruitful and increase in number; fill the earth and subdue it. Rule over the fish of the sea and the birds of the air and over every living creature that moves on the ground" (Genesis 1:27-28).

Furthermore, the Genesis account describes the first marriage and demonstrates God's hand in its creation:

> The LORD God said, "It is not good for the man to be alone. I will make a helper suitable for him." Now the LORD God had formed out of the ground all the beasts of the field and all the birds of the air. He brought them to the man to see what he would name them; and whatever the man called each living creature, that was its name. So the man gave names to all the livestock, the birds of the air and all the beasts of the field. But for Adam no suitable helper was found. So the LORD God caused the man to fall into a deep sleep; and while he was sleeping, he took one of the man's ribs and closed up the place with flesh. Then the LORD God made a woman from the rib he had taken out of the man, and he brought her to the man. The

man said, This is now bone of my bones and flesh of my flesh; she shall be called 'woman,' for she was taken out of man." For this reason a man will leave his father and mother and be united to his wife, and they will become one flesh (Genesis 2:18-24).

Jesus himself reinforces this biblical model of marriage:

"Haven't you read," he replied, "that at the beginning the Creator 'made them male and female,' and said, 'For this reason a man will leave his father and mother and be united to his wife, and the two will become one flesh'? So they are no longer two, but one. Therefore what God has joined together, let man not separate." "Why then," they asked, "did Moses command that a man give his wife a certificate of divorce and send her away?" Jesus replied, "Moses permitted you to divorce your wives because your hearts were hard. But it was not this way from the beginning" (Matthew 19:4-8).

It is clear from these verses, and many more that could be listed, that God is the author and designer of marriage. This is, of course, contrary to atheistic assertions that marriage was a human invention for the propagation of the species. It also opposes societal assertions that marriage is only a human contract.

God-Ordained Marriage

Since marriage was created, ordained, and instituted by God, it is not man's responsibility nor his right to superimpose rules or regulations concerning it. The rules and regulations that guide marriage come from God Himself. Happily for mankind, God has not left us without a clear word about this issue. The Bible is the "rule book" which gives us the rules and regulations regarding marriage. The first four rules or regulations of marriage are basic.

Rule number one is that marriage is to be monogamous. When God created mankind, He created only two humans (a man and a woman), not three or four. There were no "spares" in case the relationship between Adam and Eve did not work out. Marriage is the legal union and spiritual covenant of only two persons with God as the Third Person of the covenant. Note in the following passage, Jesus says that "a man" and "wife" are "two" who shall become "one flesh." It is not "a man" and "wives" (polygamy), nor is it "men" and "wife" (polyandry). Jesus said:

> For this reason *a man* will leave his father and mother and be united to his *wife*, and the *two* will become one flesh. So they are no longer two, but one. Therefore what God has joined together, let man not separate (emphasis mine, Matthew 19:5-6).

Rule number two is that marriage is to be heterosexual. The marriage partners must be *a man* and *a woman*. When God created mankind, He created a man and a woman. "Haven't you read," he replied, "that at the beginning the Creator 'made them male and female'" (Matthew 19:4).

Rule number three is that marriage is to be lifelong. "Therefore what God has joined together, let man not separate" (Matthew 19:6).

Rule number four is that marriage is to be the highest human relationship. The relationship of husband and wife eclipses even that of parent and child. Referring to Genesis 2:24, Jesus says, "For this reason a man *will leave his father and mother* and be united to his wife, and the two will become one flesh" (emphasis mine, Matthew 19:5).

So, God created marriage to be indissoluble in this life. Also, since the man and woman were to become "one flesh," God intended that the union of marriage be more than simply a social arrangement or a contract between two people. They are to share a common life, a common way of thinking, and a common covenant with God. These two people are to have a oneness of physical, emotional, intellectual, and spiritual being.

Polygamy and Monogamy

Even though polygamy (plural marriage) is a recognized fact of the Old Testament, the law forbade polygamy for the kings of Israel (Deuteronomy 17:17). Yet both Solomon (1 Kings 11:1-3) and David (2 Samuel 5:13) had multiple wives and much trouble as a result. Polygamy, however, was not forbidden for the average Israelite. For them, polygamy appears in Deuteronomy as an acceptable practice.

However, God's ideal marriage is an exclusive relationship of one man and one woman. When pressed by the Pharisees for an answer to the seeming divorce "command" of Moses, Jesus clearly stated that God's ideal is one of monogamy:

> "Haven't you read," he replied, "that at the beginning the Creator 'made them male and female,' and said, 'For this reason a man will leave his father and mother and be united to his wife, and the two will become one flesh'? So they are no longer two, but one. Therefore what God has joined together, let man not separate." "Why then," they asked, "did Moses command that a man give his wife a certificate of divorce and send her away?" Jesus replied, "Moses permitted you to divorce your wives because your hearts were hard. But it was not this way from the beginning" (Matthew 19:4-8).

For two people to attain a oneness of physical, emotional, intellectual, and spiritual being, they must commit themselves exclusively to one another (and to God). This ideal state of oneness cannot be attained within a polygamous relationship.

While the society described by Deuteronomy allows for polygamy, obvious difficulties arise from plural marriages. For example, jealousy is an ever-present human emotion, and it will be aroused when one of the wives feels that she or her children are less loved by her husband. This is seen in Genesis 29:15; 30:24. Jacob loved his wife Rachel more than he loved his wife Leah. Also, Jacob favored Rachel's sons, and this too resulted in family tensions.

In Old Testament theology there is an implicit favoring of monogamy. First, this is seen in the narratives of unhappy homes due to polygamy. Often there is rivalry between wives: Leah and Rachel (Genesis 30); Hannah and Peninnah (1 Samuel 1:1-6). Next, religious leaders were to be monogamous. Adam, Noah, Isaac, Joseph, Moses, and Job, each had only one wife. Also the high priests were to be monogamous (Leviticus 21:1-14). The Bible shows us that God's ideal is that marriage is to be a lifelong *monogamous* union.

Heterosexual Marriages Only

One might argue that the position of anti-homosexual-marriages is assumed within the pages of Holy Writ and need not be brought up in a study of this kind. However, the question of homosexual marriages is given treatment here because of its growing acceptance and tolerance in many human societies. Sad to say, even many church leaders have become seduced by the unbiblical notion that God is somehow in favor of same-sex marriages.

However, a God-ordained marriage is one that involves only members of the opposite sex. Jesus says as much when He says, "Haven't you read . . . that at the beginning the Creator 'made them male and female'" (Matthew 19:4). It is clear that in both the Old Testament and the New Testament, God did not intend, nor does He condone, so-called "homosexual marriages." A real marriage covenant can only be between a man and a woman. Since God himself actually joins the marriage partners together and makes them one, and since He condemns homosexuality in both the Old Testament (Leviticus 18:22) and the New Testament (Romans 1:18-27), it is impossible for a homosexual union to be a real marriage. God cannot condone what He condemns. So, whatever human societies and institutions might call a "homosexual union," one thing it can never be is a true *marriage covenant* between two marriage partners and the Third Person, the true living

God.[5]

The Marriage Covenant

Marriage is much more than simply two persons deciding to live together under the blessing of the law. As stated above, marriage is a covenant. Note these two verses:

> Because the Lord has been a witness between you and the wife of your youth . . . she is your companion and your wife by covenant (Malachi 2:14).

> That leaves the companion of her youth, and forgets the covenant of her God (Proverbs 2:17).

The Hebrew word for covenant means to be "in league with" or "a union of persons." This word is used in the Old Testament of agreements between men. David and Jonathan had a covenant. Their covenant was one of mutual protection, and it was binding upon both men's descendants forever:

> Then Jonathan made a covenant with David because he loved him as himself. . . . And Jonathan said to David, "Go in safety, inasmuch as we have sworn to each other in the name of the Lord, saying, 'The Lord will be between me and you, and between my descendants and your descendants forever'" (1 Samuel 18:3; 20:42).

In summary, the marriage covenant is a union of two persons joined together by the power of God. Marriage is an awesome responsibility. God is the Third Party and witness of the covenant. Therefore, marriage is a covenant, a solemn and binding promise made between a man and a woman, and made

[5] For fuller information on this issue, see James R. White and Jeffrey D. Niell, *The Same Sex Controversy: Defending and Clarifying the Bible's Message About Homosexuality* (Bethany House Publishers, 2002).

before and to God. It is God who joins the two together into "one flesh."

> So they are no longer two, but one. Therefore what God has joined together, let man not separate (Matthew 19:6).

Study Questions For

Chapter 3
What is Marriage?

1. What is Marriage Model # 1? Give a brief description of it.
2. What is Marriage Model # 2? Give a brief description of it.
3. What is Marriage Model # 3? Give a brief description of it.
4. Why are these three models of marriage not simply options from which people can select when they get married?
5. Where did marriage originate?
6. Should man superimpose rules or regulations upon marriage? Why or why not?
7. Name the four basic rules or regulations of marriage.
8. Briefly address the issues of polygamy and monogamy. What are they and how do they relate to a biblical view of divorce and remarriage?
9. Briefly address the fact that the Bible endorses only heterosexual marriages.
10. Briefly describe or define the word "covenant."

*Marrying for love may be a bit risky, but it is so honest
that God can't help but smile on it.—Josh Billings*

Chapter 4

God Hates Divorce

Pastor Gene Peterson told the young man, "Well, it is not God's will for you to divorce because we know that God hates divorce; Malachi 2:16 says so. Since we know that God hates divorce, then we know He doesn't want you to get a divorce."

Marshall Sellers didn't want the divorce either, but his wife left him to "find herself." Marshall and his wife, Candy, were Christians, but lately she'd been having second thoughts about being married. They had been married for nearly two years, and Candy decided she didn't like being married. Marshall was a nice guy and though he was not a perfect husband, he worked hard at supporting his new bride and showing her the love she needed. However, in spite of his efforts, she moved out of their home and found an apartment with a girlfriend in another city about 60 miles away. Pastor Peterson seemed to lay the entire burden of the separation upon Marshall as he continued his counseling sessions with him. The pastor would often give directives to Marshall that he needed to pray more, fast more, and read his Bible more. At this time in Marshall's life, other than going to work, he spent little time doing anything other than what Pastor Peterson told him to do. Included in the pastor's directives were instructions to visit Candy at her new home and attempt to "win her back." Marshall did so, but Candy had made up her mind and no matter how much he tried to talk with her, no matter how much he prayed, no matter how much he fasted, and no matter how much he read his Bible, he simply could not convince her to come home.

In due time, as with most cases like this, Candy became involved with another man, and she divorced Marshall. Oddly, Pastor Peterson seemed to be less and less available for Marshall after the divorce. As time progressed, it become painfully clear to Marshall that Pastor Peterson held him in low regard now that he was a divorcé. Ultimately the pastor made it abundantly clear that Marshall was *persona non grata*. Not only had his wife divorced him, but now Marshall felt that this Christian leader had also "divorced" him as a friend. Could it be that the pastor's theology that God hates divorce somehow transmuted into the unspoken idea that God hates the divorcé?

God Hates Divorce: The Context

In Malachi 2:16, God says: "I hate divorce." Some people have taken this passage in a universal way. In other words, they have taken it to mean that God hates all divorce equally. But does God really hate every divorce, every time, in the same way? The historical context of Malachi helps us understand what was going on in Israel at this time and the reason why God says, in this particular context, that He hates divorce.

During this time in history, the men of Israel were divorcing their wives simply to marry foreign women. Presumably, these women were not just foreigners but most likely younger and more beautiful than the Israelite wives. Note Malachi 2:11-12:

> Judah has broken faith. A detestable thing has been committed in Israel and in Jerusalem: Judah has desecrated the sanctuary the LORD loves, by marrying the daughter of a foreign god. As for the man who does this, whoever he may be, may the LORD cut him off from the tents of Jacob—even though he brings offerings to the LORD Almighty.

What was going on in Malachi's day was a sort of male mid-life crisis. In Malachi 2:11, the prophet reprimands the men for their mixed-faith marriages. Furthermore, the context of this passage implies that these mixed-faith marriages had come at the cost of "treacherous" divorces. In verse 14, Malachi says that, "the Lord has been a witness between thee and the wife of thy youth, against whom thou hast dealt treacherously" (KJV). These men had no justifiable reason to divorce their wives and marry other women. Note well that when a man divorces his spouse for no justifiable reason, God says that he is violating a covenant (KJV) or has broken faith (NIV):

> You ask, "Why?" It is because the LORD is acting as the witness between you and the wife of your youth, because you have broken faith with her, though she is your partner, the wife of your marriage covenant. Has not the LORD made them one? In flesh and spirit they are his. And why one? Because he was seeking godly offspring. So guard yourself in your spirit, and do not break faith with the wife of your youth (Malachi 2:14-15).

This, then, is the kind of divorce that God says that He hates:

> "I hate divorce," says the LORD God of Israel, "and I hate a man's covering himself with violence as well as with his garment," says the LORD Almighty. So guard yourself in your spirit, and do not break faith (Malachi 2:16).

Clearly, the context of Malachi 2:16 indicates that many Israelite men were divorcing their wives to marry pagan women. God condemned this as *treacherous*. Thus, what God hates is this kind of frivolous divorcing so that the man can take another woman as his wife. Looking both at this context and other passages in the Bible that speak of divorce, it is apparent that Malachi 2:16 does not condemn all divorce equally.

Jesus himself said "that anyone who divorces his wife, *except for marital unfaithfulness*, and marries another woman commits adultery" (emphasis mine, Matthew 19:9; see also Matthew 5:32). Since Jesus acknowledged that *marital unfaithfulness* is a justifiable reason for a scriptural divorce, then God cannot hate all divorce in the same way. Rather, in Matthew 5:32 and 19:9, it would be the adultery of the unfaithful spouse that God would hate.

If God hates all divorce equally, then how could He have divorced Israel (Jeremiah 3:8a)? Furthermore, in the book of Ezra, there was a situation that had led the prophet of God to demand that the Israelites divorce their wives.

> While Ezra was praying and confessing, weeping and throwing himself down before the house of God, a large crowd of Israelites—men, women and children—gathered around him. They too wept bitterly. Then Shecaniah son of Jehiel, one of the descendants of Elam, said to Ezra, "We have been unfaithful to our God by marrying foreign women from the peoples around us. But in spite of this, there is still hope for Israel. Now let us make a covenant before our God to send away all these women and their children, in accordance with the counsel of my lord and of those who fear the commands of our God. Let it be done according to the Law" (Ezra 10:1-3).

What is surprising is that in this passage God not only condones divorce through His prophet Ezra, He demands it!

> Rise up; this matter is in your hands. We will support you, so take courage and do it." So Ezra rose up and put the leading priests and Levites and all Israel under oath to do what had been suggested. And they took the oath. Then Ezra withdrew from before the house of God and went to the room of Jehohanan son of Eliashib. While he was there, he ate no food and drank

no water, because he continued to mourn over the unfaithfulness of the exiles. A proclamation was then issued throughout Judah and Jerusalem for all the exiles to assemble in Jerusalem. Anyone who failed to appear within three days would forfeit all his property, in accordance with the decision of the officials and elders, and would himself be expelled from the assembly of the exiles. Within the three days, all the men of Judah and Benjamin had gathered in Jerusalem. And on the twentieth day of the ninth month, all the people were sitting in the square before the house of God, greatly distressed by the occasion and because of the rain. Then Ezra the priest stood up and said to them, "You have been unfaithful; you have married foreign women, adding to Israel's guilt. Now make confession to the LORD, the God of your fathers, and do his will. Separate yourselves from the peoples around you and from your foreign wives." The whole assembly responded with a loud voice: "You are right! We must do as you say." So the exiles did as was proposed. Ezra the priest selected men who were family heads, one from each family division, and all of them designated by name. On the first day of the tenth month they sat down to investigate the cases, and by the first day of the first month they finished dealing with all the men who had married foreign women. . . . (They all gave their hands in pledge to put away their wives, and for their guilt they each presented a ram from the flock as a guilt offering) (Ezra 10:4-12, 16-17, 19).

In this extraordinary situation, not only did many of the Israelite men divorce their wives at the prophet's direction, but they also sent their children away as well.

As stated earlier, we cannot accept one passage to the exclusion of another passage. So, while God does say in Malachi that He hates divorce, we must not "divorce" that statement from all of the other statements that God has made about divorce. It is clear, then, that God does not hate all divorce, and the divorce that He does hate (in Malachi) is a treacherous divorce predicated upon nothing more than the husband's libidinous desires. This type of divorce is called treacherous and has no grounds for justification. The wives whom these men were divorcing had not committed adultery. These men simply decided to "send away" their wives because they had found other, more appealing women. This is treacherous, and God states unequivocally that He hates it. But, it is bad logic and bad theology to extrapolate from this one passage that God hates all divorce equally and for the same reasons. To extract the phrase "I hate divorce" from its biblical and historical contexts and make a universal application from it is simply wrong.

What God Hath Joined Together

As has been established earlier, God's intention was that marriage be indissoluble. Jesus, in confirmation of this ideal, states that when two people come together in the marriage covenant relationship, they become one flesh: "What therefore God has joined together, let no man separate" (Matthew 19:6). The question naturally arises, "Does God join all marriages?" This is a valid question, but the center of attention is off target. For the passage does not say that God joins "marriage" but that He joins people. He joins together a man and a woman. When a man and a woman make the commitment of marriage, then God joins them together as one flesh. And of that one flesh Jesus commands that no one should separate. Jesus' statement also implies (as was discussed above) that marriage is not simply a legal contract between two people but a covenant between three individuals: the man and woman and God Himself, as the "spiritual surgeon," who joins together the two into one flesh. This one flesh concept is first pictured in Adam and Eve.

Adam and Eve were not originally two separate people. Thus, though "they" (after Eve was created) could be geographically separated, they were still one flesh. This oneness is what God brings a man and woman into when they are joined in marriage. Woman was originally taken "from" man, and in marriage God places her back "with" man. Just as the Church is both *body* and *bride* of Christ, so the woman becomes both *body* and *bride* of the man. Ephesians 5:21-31 describes this truth in picturesque terms.

> Submit to one another out of reverence for Christ. Wives, submit to your husbands as to the Lord. For the husband is the head of the wife as Christ is the head of the church, his body, of which he is the Savior. Now as the church submits to Christ, so also wives should submit to their husbands in everything. Husbands, love your wives, just as Christ loved the church and gave himself up for her to make her holy, cleansing her by the washing with water through the word, and to present her to himself as a radiant church, without stain or wrinkle or any other blemish, but holy and blameless. In this same way, husbands ought to love their wives as their own bodies. He who loves his wife loves himself. After all, no one ever hated his own body, but he feeds and cares for it, just as Christ does the church—for we are members of his body. "For this reason a man will leave his father and mother and be united to his wife, and the two will become one flesh" (Ephesians 5:21-31).

That is not to imply that only the woman becomes one with the man, for the man becomes one with the woman as well. So the woman does not simply lose her identity and become subjugated and subsumed by the man's identity; rather, the two become one. Together, they have a new identity. This interwoven intricacy is wrought by God, and all are commanded, even warned, not to break this holy union.

Old Testament Legislation of Divorce

The Old Testament clearly recognizes the fact of divorce. It was happening. Because it was happening and people were getting hurt, God gave laws to regulate it. Simply put, God accepted people where they were, but He also put restrictions on their wrong practices. Interestingly, the restriction or regulation concerning divorce in Deuteronomy seems to have been a protection clause for the woman.

> 1 If a man marries a woman who becomes displeasing to him because he finds something indecent about her, and he writes her a certificate of divorce, gives it to her and sends her from his house,
>
> 2 and if after she leaves his house she becomes the wife of another man,
>
> 3 and her second husband dislikes her and writes her a certificate of divorce, gives it to her and sends her from his house, or if he dies,
>
> 4 then her first husband, who divorced her, is not allowed to marry her again after she has been defiled. That would be detestable in the eyes of the LORD. Do not bring sin upon the land the LORD your God is giving you as an inheritance (Deuteronomy 24:1-4).

The restriction portion of this passage is located in verse 4. Verses 1-3 simply document what it was that hardhearted men were doing. Note the conditionals in this passage set off by the word "if" and the repetitious use of the word "and," and then there is the concluding conditional set off by the word "then":

If a man marries a woman who becomes displeasing to him . . .

and he writes her a certificate of divorce . . .

and sends her from his house . . .

and if after she leaves his house she becomes the wife of another man . . .

and her second husband writes her a certificate of divorce . . .

and sends her from his house, or if he dies . . .

then her first husband, who divorced her, is not allowed to marry her again . . .

The *then* of verse 4 is the beginning of the restriction or regulation. *Then the first husband cannot remarry the woman.*

This remarriage restriction protects the woman from a divorce hastily initiated by, perhaps, an angry or capricious husband. If a man could not remarry his former wife because she had married someone else, it would make him think twice about the whole matter. In other words, without the prohibition of remarriage after the ex-wife had married someone else, a husband might divorce his wife thinking, "If I'm not happy with my new wife, I can always remarry my first wife later." However, with the "no remarriage clause" after a second marriage, the man would have to evaluate the situation more thoughtfully before hastily divorcing his wife. He would think twice before putting her through the shame and humiliation of the whole episode and possibly losing her forever. Thus, due to the restriction that God (through Moses) placed on remarriage, the woman was protected from reckless mistreatment. The remarriage regulation restricted foul play on the part of the man.

It is important to understand that Moses did not all of a sudden come up with the allowance of divorce and remarriage so that men could divorce their wives. The reason Moses came up with these restrictions was that men were already divorcing their wives. And then, to make matters worse, in many cases these men would divorce their second wives and induce their former wives away from their second husbands and then remarry them. What bedlam! What lawlessness! The marriage covenant was not being held as sacred. In essence what Moses was saying by enacting these laws was, "Enough!"

It appears, then, that Moses' restriction on remarriage was introduced to rein in the sins of serial divorce and remarriages that were already going on. Moses' restriction on remarriage was instituted precisely because men were already in the habit of (1) divorcing their wives and when they thought better of it, they would (2) divorce their most recent wives, (3) induce their former wives away from their second husbands and then (4) remarry them. One can imagine the societal mayhem and confusion this would cause, not to mention the emotional pain and humiliation for the wives and their children.

So, prior to Moses' divorce-and-remarriage restriction, it appears that divorce and remarriage was out of control. But now, with this new restriction on serial marriages, divorces, and remarriages, a husband would have to thoughtfully consider the possible irrevocable consequences. He would have to be certain that he did not want his wife back before he casually divorced her. With this new restriction now placed on remarriage, a divorce could very well be final.

Moses and Divorce

It is important to realize and understand that while God permitted divorce, under certain circumstances, He did not prescribe it (except in the case of Ezra). The Pharisees missed this altogether and thought that Moses had *commanded* divorce for certain situations. So, when Jesus reiterated God's ideal, they asked him, "Why then did Moses *command* to give her a certificate and divorce her?" (emphasis mine, Matthew 19:7). Jesus made it clear to them however that Moses only *permitted* divorce, and that it was permitted only because of the hardness of their hearts. Yet even this permission was not for "any cause at all" (Matthew 19:3) as was the common thought and practice of the day.

A Certificate of Divorce

I gave a pre-exam to some students in a class on divorce and remarriage. (A pre-exam on the first day of class helps me assess how much students know about the topic when we begin the class.) One of the questions on the pre-exam was, "Why did Moses allow a man to give his wife a certificate of divorce?" One of the women in the class didn't have a clue as to the correct answer, so she thought she'd be funny and she wrote, "So that she could frame it and hang it on her wall."

When I read her answer to the class, everyone had a good laugh. However, after the laughter was over, no one was more shocked than the woman who had written that answer when I announced that she was correct.

A Certificate of Explanation

You see, men were divorcing their wives because of the hardness of their hearts (Matthew 19:3). What Moses did was put in place a protection for the woman by requiring the man to give her a "certificate of divorce" (i.e., a certificate of explanation) that explained *why* he was divorcing her. If a man was divorcing his wife because he found another woman that he liked better, then his ex-wife had a certificate which she could show others that made it clear that she had not done anything wrong.

Too often people would immediately think the worst of those who were divorced. If they met a woman who was divorced, they might think to themselves, "I wonder what horrible thing she did that *forced* her husband to divorce her." However, with the "certificate of divorce," she had a written document (certificate of explanation) to show others that it was not her fault.

In that day, men would often divorce their wives for almost any reason. If a wife burned her husband's meal, he might divorce her. So, if she "burnt his toast," he'd write a certificate of divorce explaining why he was divorcing her: "She burnt my toast." He'd put the certificate of divorce in her hand and "send her away." Then, if another man was interested in her, she could show him the certificate of divorce, and he would know why ("burnt toast") she was divorced. He could read for himself that the former husband was the irresponsible party.

For What Reason?

We know what the *certificate of divorce* was (i.e., certificate of explanation). We know what its purpose was (for the protection of the woman). However, *for what reason* did Moses allow a man to divorce his wife? This is actually a rather difficult question to answer.

The answer to this question is an enigma, and I believe

it shall always remain so. The answer hinges upon the obscure Hebrew idiom *erwat dabar* found in Deuteronomy 24:1. According to various scholars, this term is not hard to translate, but it is difficult, if not impossible, to interpret. An agreed upon translation is "a matter of nakedness." But what does that mean? Some have suggested that it is anything and everything a husband might not like about his wife, including cooking a bad meal ("burnt toast"). Others think it is something more serious, something shameful, having to do with sexual immorality, but less than adultery. The Hebrew term *erwat dabar* is used in connection with uncovered excrement in Deuteronomy 23:12-14, Noah's nakedness in Genesis 9:21-23, and Edom under the figure of a drunken woman in Lamentations 4:21. Still others have argued that Moses certainly would not have permitted divorce for anything less than adultery; therefore, the Hebrew term *erwat dabar* must mean adultery. So, the interpretation of the Hebrew term *erwat dabar* runs the gamut from "burnt toast" to adultery. We could go on giving other contemporary interpretations, but the point is made: *erwat debar* is very difficult to interpret, and good, conservative, biblical scholars disagree on the interpretation of this term.

Hillel and Shammai

Understanding an ancient Hebrew idiom is indeed difficult for us since we have so many years (not to mention differences in laws and culture) from the time of Moses to our own. The exact meaning that Moses had in mind has been lost to us. But, interestingly, the exact meaning of this idiom was apparently lost even to the Jews themselves by the time of Christ.

The ambiguity of the term *erwat debar* was a factor in the two rabbinic schools of thought that had arisen by the time of Jesus. These two schools were that of Hillel and Shammai. Hillel and his followers were very liberal in their interpretation of what *erwat debar* meant in Deuteronomy 24:1-4. Hillel taught that *erwat debar* referred to anything that displeased the husband. This could range from cooking a bad meal to flirtatious behavior on the part of the wife. It could include violations of the law or Jewish customs. It could include a woman exposing her arms in public. It could even include the wife appearing in public with her hair messed up.

The school of Shammai, however, was much more conservative in its interpretation of *erwat debar*. This school taught that *erwat debar* referred to unfaithfulness in the marriage; it was some serious sexual sin.

But who was correct? Would Moses allow a man to give his wife a certificate of divorce for "burning his toast"? Or, would Moses only have allowed a man to give his wife a certificate of divorce for adultery?

Not Adultery

It seems reasonably clear that *erwat debar* did not refer to adultery. According to the laws of the Jews at the time of Moses, death by stoning—and not a certificate of divorce—was the prescribed punishment for adultery. Thus, it seems apparent that *erwat debar* could not have meant adultery because for that offense, the law required capital punishment; therefore, it must have meant something less than adultery.

So, while we can be reasonably certain that *erwat debar* did not mean adultery, we also know that our theology on divorce does not rest solely on this Hebrew idiom.

At this stage of our investigation, the main point that we need to glean from Deuteronomy 24:1-4 is that divorce and remarriage were common practices among God's people. God's law allowed for and regulated divorce and remarriage due to something less than adultery.

What precisely was meant by *erwat debar* is uncertain, but our main concern is not the interpretation of *erwat debar*. Our main concern is Jesus' words and the rest of the New Testament. People today who are facing divorce situations and desiring to know the biblical position are not at the mercy of the ambiguous phrase *erwat debar*. Jesus ended the debate of interpretations and has clearly spoken to the issue. The Apostle Paul has also given us God's Word on these issues.

Study Questions For

Chapter 4
God Hates Divorce

1. What is the context of God's statement, "I hate divorce." And, why is context important?
2. What does the author mean when he says: "Some people have taken this passage ('I hate divorce,' Malachi 2:16) in a universal way."
3. Does God hate every divorce, every time, in the same way?
4. Does Malachi 2:16 condemn all divorce equally?
5. In Matthew 19:9 and also in Matthew 5:32, Jesus acknowledged that marital unfaithfulness is a justifiable reason for a scriptural divorce. How does this coincide with God's statement, "I hate divorce" in Malachi 2:16?
6. If God hates all divorce equally, then how could He have divorced Israel (Jeremiah 3:8a)?
7. God condoned divorce through His prophet Ezra, but did He actually command it? Give Scripture.
8. What does the author intend to convey when he says, "we cannot accept one passage to the exclusion of another passage."
9. What was the purpose of the remarriage restriction in Deuteronomy 24:4?
10. Why did Moses impose a restriction on serial marriages, divorces, and remarriages?
11. Why did Moses allow a man to give his wife a certificate of divorce?
12. For what reasons did Moses allow a man to divorce his wife?
13. Discuss the obscure Hebrew idiom *erwat dabar* found in Deuteronomy 24:1.
14. Who were Hillel and Shammai?
15. Why does the author say that it seems reasonably clear that *erwat debar* did not refer to adultery?
16. What is the main point that we need to glean from Deuteronomy 24:1-4 at this stage of our investigation?

When a man opens a car door for his wife,
it's either a new car or a new wife.—Prince Philip

Chapter 5

Paul on Divorce

But to the rest I say, not the Lord, that if any brother has a wife who is an unbeliever, and she consents to live with him, let him not send her away. And a woman who has an unbelieving husband, and he consents to live with her, let her not send her husband away (1 Corinthians 7:12-13).

A woman came to my office and in sheer exasperation said, "I want to divorce my non-Christian husband." I sat up in my chair and gave her my full attention. I asked, "Why do you want to divorce him?" She said, "Because I have fallen out of love with him." I sat there for a moment expecting more to the answer, but none came. So, I asked, "What is it that he has done to cause you to fall out of love with him?" She responded by saying:

Oh, I don't know . . . a thousand little things really. I can't stand the way he sucks air through his teeth after he eats. I've told him a million times to simply go to the bathroom and brush his teeth. He also has this annoying habit of humming in the shower, and it drives me nuts. And if he's not at work, he's always home. I never have any alone time. I've got friends whose husbands at least stop off at a bar with their buddies for a couple of beers, but not him! After work, he comes straight home and starts playing with our baby.

The conversation went on from there, and the more she talked, the better she made her husband sound. This was a nice man who loved his family, worked hard, paid the bills, and spent quality time with his child. I kept expecting her to say that she had caught him with another woman or that he had been frequenting a prostitute, but no. Finally, I opened the Bible to 1 Corinthians 7:12-13 and read the passage to her.

She looked at me with an almost frightened expression and said, "You mean that as long as he wants to stay married to me, I have to stay married to him?" I said, "Well, these are the words of the Apostle Paul, and he was writing under the inspiration of the Holy Spirit, so these are God's words."

"But wait," she went on, "didn't he just say that these were his words and not God's words?"

Paul's Words are God's Words

In this passage, Paul makes an interesting distinction. He says, "I, not the Lord, say." So, if it is just Paul who is saying something about this topic, why is it incumbent upon Christians to listen and obey? After all, he says that it is *he* and not the Lord speaking.

There have been questions about the fact that Paul makes a distinction between what it is that *the Lord says* and what it is that *he says*. Because of that distinction, some have suggested that what Paul says in this verse is not inspired Scripture. However, before we jump to that conclusion, let's look at a possible reason for Paul making such a distinction.

All through the book of Romans, Paul quotes from the Old Testament to "prove" his points. Galatians is another masterpiece of this type of strategy. In some quarters of the Christian community, they would say that Paul gave "chapter and verse." Paul does this with all of his theology. Thus, he could be expected to quote "chapter and verse," or Jesus himself concerning the subject of divorce and remarriage, and this he does.

In 1 Corinthians 7:10 Paul wrote: "And unto the married I command, *yet not I, but the Lord,* let not the wife depart from her husband" (emphasis mine). Paul says that he received that word from the Lord (cf. Matthew 5:32; 19:9; Mark 10:11; Luke 16:18). As long as Jesus had given guidelines and laws concerning divorce and remarriage, Paul was obligated to quote Him. But when there was something concerning the subject of divorce and remarriage that Jesus had not expressly dealt with, Paul, as an inspired writer of Holy Writ, would have to pen guidelines for such instances. This is exactly what I believe he does in 1 Corinthians 7:12-13. In verse 12a Paul says, "But to the rest *I* say, not the Lord." I do not believe that Paul is saying that what he is about to teach is not *from* God. What he is saying is that there is no *precedent*, no *previous word* from God to quote on this subject. Therefore, by the unction and inspiration of the Holy Spirit, he will now write. Paul's "I say" is inspired Scripture on par with any and all other Scripture throughout the Bible. With that distinction Paul's teaching on the subject of divorce is made clearer. Paul's words are God's Word.

No Divorce for Christian Couples

Speaking to *Christian couples,* Paul says that the wife is not to separate from her husband, and a husband is not to divorce his wife. Simply stated: Christian couples are not to divorce.

> To the married I give this command (not I, but the Lord): A wife must not separate from her husband. But if she does, she must remain unmarried or else be reconciled to her husband. And a husband must not divorce his wife (1 Corinthians 7:10-11).

Paul gives this directive undoubtedly upon the authority of Jesus' own words (Matthew 5:32; 19:9; Mark 10:11; Luke 16:18). Being a realist, Paul recognized that even though there was a clear word from Jesus on the issue, i.e., no divorce, there were still some Christians who were getting divorced. So it is a fact: divorce *does* happen among believers.

Finding himself in a very similar situation to Moses' situation centuries earlier, Paul was attempting to put restrictions on what believers *were already doing*. Paul says that Christians should not divorce, *but if they do*, then both the husband and the wife are to remain single allowing for the possibility of reconciliation. A believer is not to divorce his or her spouse. If, however, Christians do divorce, they have only two options: Verse 11: (1) *they can remain unmarried*, or (2) *they can be reconciled.*

Next, in verse 11b Paul says, "Let not the husband put away his wife." Paul was not talking about adultery here. He was dealing with how a Christian couple should view their marriage: no divorce.

In summary, Paul says that there is to be no divorce for a Christian couple, but if a Christian couple does divorce, they are not free to remarry, other than to remarry each other.

Christians Forbidden to Initiate
Divorce from Unbelievers

After speaking to the Christian couples, Paul shifts his attention to "the rest."

> But to the rest I say, not the Lord, that if any brother has a wife who is an unbeliever, and she consents to live with him, let him not send her away. And a woman who has an unbelieving husband, and he consents to live with her, let her not send her husband away (1 Corinthians 7:12-13).

As Christianity spread, more and more people were converted, but the spouses of these new converts did not always become Christians themselves. Consequently, many Christians were married to unbelieving spouses. This is something that had not been dealt with in previous New Testament times. Jesus had not dealt with this situation (mixed-marriages, i.e., *believer and nonbeliever*) in his teaching because during his incarnation, his ministry was almost exclusively limited to issues within Judaism. Therefore, Paul is now called upon as an apostle (i.e., special messenger of Christ) and a writer of inspired Scripture to deal with "the rest," the believer-unbeliever mixed marriages. Thus, the rest are believers married to unbelievers.

It appears from what it is that Paul has to say to this particular group that the Corinthians had asked him specifically about several issues, one of which was mixed-marriages. Paul's writing was in response to specific questions that the Corinthians had asked him in a letter. He says, "Now for the matters you wrote about" (1 Corinthians 7:1a). It appears that a question some of the Corinthian believers were asking was, "Does marriage to a nonbeliever defile the believer and the children?" According to Paul's heritage, for a Jew to be married to a Gentile was to defile oneself and the offspring. Thus, one might expect him to answer the Corinthians' question by saying, "Yes, it does defile." But, Paul does not say that. In fact, he says just the opposite: "For the unbelieving husband is sanctified through his wife, and the unbelieving wife is sanctified through her husband; for otherwise your children are unclean, but now they are holy" (1 Corinthians 7:14). It appears that one Christian parent is enough to make a Christian home. Paul gives two reasons why Christians should stay in a mixed-marriage situation: (a) The unbelieving spouse is sanctified by the believing spouse, and (b) the children are sanctified by the presence of the Christian parent. (This is not to say "saved." Each person must come to Jesus Christ personally for salvation, Romans 10:9-10.) Upon this basis Paul says that a Christian is not to initiate a divorce.

> . . . if any brother has a wife who is an unbeliever, and she consents to live with him, *let him not send her away*. And a woman who has an unbelieving husband, and he consents to live with her, *let her not send her husband away* (emphasis mine, 1 Corinthians 7:12-13).

If a believer is married to an unbeliever and the unbeliever is content to remain in the marriage, then the Christian is obligated by the covenant of marriage to remain married to the unbeliever.

If the Unbeliever Departs

Paul goes on, however, to give different instructions for those Christians whose unbelieving spouses want a divorce. "Yet if the unbelieving one leaves, let him leave; the brother or the sister is not under bondage in such cases, but God has called us to peace" (1 Corinthians 7:15). It is surprising to some that Paul says that the Christian may allow an unbelieving partner to get a divorce if that is what the unbeliever wants. Many today tell Christians that if their unbelieving spouse wants a divorce, they should fight tooth and nail to keep their spouse from leaving. But Paul says, if the unbelieving spouse decides to leave and thus break the marriage covenant, let him/her go.

There has been some question as to how to interpret the partner leaving. Some have suggested that something less than legal divorce is intended. Others believe that what is meant in this passage by the leaving of the unsaved spouse is in fact a legal divorce. Keeping a solid view of the context, it appears this passage is referring to the concept of a legal divorce, as was the custom of the day. The key is that the *unbeliever has voluntarily initiated the divorce*. The believer does not "send the spouse away," but rather the unbeliever chooses to divorce the believer. Thus, if an unbelieving partner insists on divorcing his or her spouse, it is a legal divorce, and "A believing man or woman is not bound in such circumstances" (1 Corinthians 7:15b).

The next question naturally follows: What does it mean that the Christian is "not under bondage"? Does it simply mean that the believer is no longer obligated to the previous marriage, or does it also include the freedom to remarry? This question and its answer will be discussed later. For now, we recognize that the Apostle Paul, under the inspiration of the Holy Spirit, regulated divorce.

Study Questions For

Chapter 5
Paul on Divorce

1. Paul says, "But to the rest I say, not the Lord" (1 Corinthians 7:12). What does the author say about this?
2. Does Paul say that Christian couples can divorce?
3. Paul says if a Christian couple does divorce, both the husband and the wife are to do what?
4. Is a Christian allowed to initiate a divorce from an unbeliever who does not want a divorce? Give Scripture.
5. What should the Christian do if his/her unbelieving spouse wants a divorce?

*For this reason a man will leave his father and mother and
be united to his wife, and the two will become one flesh.
So they are no longer two, but one.—Jesus Christ*

Chapter 6

Jesus on Divorce

Desire-Beliefs

Tammy sat in the chair across from the counselor and
said, "I don't believe it. It's simply not true."

Tammy's worried brother had followed her husband
and secretly video taped him going in and out of bars and hotel
rooms with other women. Silhouetted in the night's light was
Thad hugging and kissing other women. Tammy's brother
was not able to get video of Thad's actions behind closed
doors; one could only imagine.

The video was shocking and overwhelming evidence
that Thad was having multiple affairs. When Tammy
confronted Thad, he denied that it was him. Because the video
was filmed at night, there was never a clear picture of Thad's
face. However, it was clear enough for any objective person to
recognize him. The subject in the video wore Thad's type of
clothing. It was his general body type, hair cut, and more. His
car was filmed up close and the license plate was zoomed-in
on. No doubt about it. It was his car, and someone who looked
identical to Thad was driving it, and getting in and out of it
with other women.

However, Thad had a convenient answer. Incredible as
it was, he said that he had loaned his car and his coat to a
buddy of his so his friend could be with other women. Thad
maintained that he hadn't committed adultery; he had only
helped his buddy commit adultery. When asked who the other

guy was, Thad had a convenient answer ready: he said that he couldn't reveal that because he didn't want to get his friend into trouble. In spite of the video tape, her brother's personal eyewitness testimony, and testimony from others who knew Thad, Tammy chose to believe Thad. As staggering as it all was, Tammy simply believed what she wanted to be true.

We've all met people who knew something was probably not true, but they desired it to be true. So, they just believed that it was true. I call these types of beliefs, "desire-beliefs." Desire-beliefs are by definition wrong beliefs.

Humans are interesting and curious beings. One of the many curious things that we have the ability to do is believe something because *we want it to be true*. We have the ability to do the opposite as well. We can choose not to believe something because *we do not want it to be true*.

I was once witnessing to a man about the Lord. We had talked about salvation in Christ, and heaven and hell. He was not a believer, and I was hoping that he'd find Christ as his Savior. Then, in an interesting twist, he turned to me and said, "Well, Rick, what you have to remember is that I don't believe in hell, so I'm not going there." Stunned for a second, I quickly realized that he had simply chosen not to believe in hell, and through his desire-belief he had convinced himself that it didn't exist. I responded by telling him that hell's existence was not contingent upon his belief. The shocked look on his face was telling, so I followed up and said: "You see, hell is real whether you believe it is or not."

It seems that almost all parents have desire-beliefs about their children. They know, logically, that their kids are not perfect, but many of them have the incredible ability to ignore the facts and believe what it is that they *want* to be true. How many times have parents said, "No! Johnny could not have done that. It must have been those other boys that he runs around with!" I've seen parents take the dubious word of their kid who was in trouble over a well-meaning adult who had nothing to gain by lying about the situation. As a counselor for many years, I cannot count the number of times I have encountered people with strong desire-beliefs in spite of what appeared to be overwhelming evidence to the contrary.

Being that we are fallen humans, it is altogether likely that all of us have some desire-beliefs. However, we must be careful not to allow our desire-beliefs to dictate our theology.

Jesus, Desire-Beliefs, and Divorce

There is a persistent desire-belief with regard to Jesus and divorce. Some people see divorce as so sinful (due to faulty information and bad research) that they cannot fathom the idea that Jesus would ever allow it in any way, shape, or form. Thus, they desire that Jesus always denounce divorce in every situation. I received a kind-spirited e-mail from a man who held firmly to this desire-belief. He wrote to me to let me know that he disagreed with my theology on divorce and remarriage. He had read an article that I had written on this topic, and he wrote:

> In your article you said that Jesus allows for divorce in cases of infidelity, but I do not believe that to be the case. The Bible uses the word fornication *only* in times when it refers to two people, *neither of whom are married* who have sex. It *never* refers to adultery as fornication. *What I believe* Jesus is saying is that if when you are married you believe that your spouse is a virgin and you find out differently, then you may divorce her.

Just as Tammy simply desired and thus chose to believed that Thad would not have an affair, this man desired that Jesus never allow divorce. His desire-belief had simply blinded him to several pertinent facts about the word *fornication* as it is found in the *King James Version* of the Bible. But he is not alone. Many Christians share his misunderstanding of the word *fornication*.

The Believer May Initiate Divorce

So, did Jesus ever allow grounds for divorce? Yes, He did make clear a situation when it is permissible for a believer to initiate a divorce. This situation is predicated upon that which has often been called *the exception clause* (see Matthew 5:32 and 19:9). Jesus states unequivocally that it is unlawful to divorce one's spouse *except* for fornication (Matthew 5:32; 19:9, KJV). So, Jesus does permit a Christian to initiate a divorce when there is fornication on the part of the other spouse. However, what is this word "fornication"? What does it mean?

Fornication Defined

Since Jesus explicitly allowed for the initiation of divorce on the grounds of *fornication*, it is imperative to discover what this term means. The word *fornication* is simply the English translation of the Greek word *porneia*.

The *Amplified Bible* version translates *fornication* as "unfaithfulness (sexual immorality)."

> But I tell you, Whoever dismisses and repudiates and divorces his wife, except on the grounds of unfaithfulness (sexual immorality), causes her to commit adultery, and whoever marries a woman who has been divorced commits adultery (Matthew 5:32, *Amplified Bible*).

The *New International Version* translates it as "marital unfaithfulness."

> But I tell you that anyone who divorces his wife, except for marital unfaithfulness, causes her to become an adulteress, and anyone who marries the divorced woman commits adultery (Matthew 5:32, NIV).

The *New American Standard Bible* translates it "unchastity."

> but I say to you that everyone who divorces his wife, except for the reason of unchastity, makes her commit adultery; and whoever marries a divorced woman commits adultery (Matthew 5:32, NASB).

In our modern-day English, the word *fornication* has a narrow meaning. Today, fornication is understood to be sexual relations between unmarried persons (by consent of each). Since this is the case, fornication is commonly seen as different from adultery because fornication does not involve married persons.

Semantic Anachronism

When the *King James Version* of the Bible was written, about four hundred years ago, the English word *fornication* did not have the narrow definition that it has today. At that time, it was used to mean any kind of sexual immorality, including but not limited to sexual promiscuity, prostitution, and adultery. We commit the fallacy of semantic anachronism (a definition out of time) when we read our narrow, modern-day definition of the word *fornication* back into the Bible.

Anyone who has done even a little study in languages knows that the meanings of words can (and often do) change with use. The word *fornication* is just such a word. To help make this point, let's look at a couple of other words that the *King James* translators used that have since changed meanings.

Quick

What does it mean to be "quick"? Well, our modern-day dictionaries say that it means something like, "moving fast." However, four hundred years ago the word meant "alive" and "living." Let's compare a few passages in the KJV and the NIV.

Compare Numbers 16:30 in the KJV and the NIV:

> But if the LORD make a new thing, and the earth open her mouth, and swallow them up, with all that appertain unto them, and they go down *quick* into the pit; then ye shall understand that these men have provoked the LORD (emphasis mine, KJV).

But if the LORD brings about something totally new, and the earth opens its mouth and swallows them, with everything that belongs to them, and they go down *alive* into the grave, then you will know that these men have treated the LORD with contempt (emphasis mine, NIV).

Compare Psalm 55:15 in the KJV and the NIV.

Let death seize upon them, and let them go down *quick* into hell: for wickedness is in their dwellings, and among them (emphasis mine, KJV).

Let death take my enemies by surprise; let them go down *alive* to the grave, for evil finds lodging among them (emphasis mine, NIV).

Compare Acts 10:42 in the KJV and the NIV.

And he commanded us to preach unto the people, and to testify that it is he which was ordained of God to be the Judge of *quick* and dead (emphasis mine, KJV).

He commanded us to preach to the people and to testify that he is the one whom God appointed as judge of the *living* and the dead (emphasis mine, NIV).

Can you imagine a youth pastor trying to get his youth members to drive more safely using the *King James Version* of Acts 10:42 as his text? It might go something like this:

Listen up kids, especially you boys with fast cars. You must be careful not to drive over the speed limit. Remember, the Bible says that God is the "Judge of *quick* and dead," and if you keep driving quick, you'll end up dead, and then God will judge you for driving too fast.

We may smile at such a foolish notion, but when people read their modern-day definitions back into the Bible, all sorts of foolishness is taught and preached.

Kine

Next, what is "kine"? It's a word that has dropped out of use since the KJV was written (i.e., semantic obsolescence). Kine is the plural of cow (i.e., cows). See Genesis 41:1-32 in the KJV concerning the story of the Pharaoh's dream of the fat and skinny "kine" (cows).

Prevent

And, what do we think the word "prevent" means? Well, in modern-day English, it means "to keep from happening." To stop something. However, in 1 Thessalonians 4:15, the KJV Bible says, "For this we say unto you by the Word of the Lord, that we which are alive and remain unto the coming of the Lord *shall not prevent* them which are asleep" (emphasis mine).

Why would we want to "prevent them which are asleep"? And, what would we want to prevent them from doing anyway? Again, we must be careful not to read our *modern-day* definition back into the biblical text. When the KJV was written, the word "prevent" meant "precede" or "go before." The NIV clarifies this passage with this translation: "According to the Lord's own word, we tell you that we who are still alive, who are left till the coming of the Lord, will certainly not *precede* those who have fallen asleep" (emphasis mine, 1 Thessalonians 4:15). In other words, when the Lord comes for His church, the dead in Christ will rise first, and then those Christians who are alive will be raptured.

Simply stated: Christians must not take modern-day definitions and read those definitions back into the biblical text. When people do this, it causes all sorts of interpretive disasters.

So, now, with that background, it's really quite simple: four hundred years ago the word *fornication* simply did not mean what it means today.

Just like the word *quick* means something different to us than it did four hundred years ago, and just like the word *prevent* means something different to us than it did four hundred years ago, so too the word *fornication* means something different to us than it did four hundred years ago. If we are honest about this fact, we will not read our modern-day definition of *fornication* back into the Bible.

The History of the Word Fornication

Again, remember that the word fornication (like many other English words) has undergone meaning change over the years. In fact, I was reading an exchange on the Internet about the issue of sexual immorality and Christians, and I ran across this dialog:

> **New Christian:** "In the KJV Bible, God clearly states that 'fornication' is not permitted. But, I don't know what 'fornication' is. Can someone help me understand?"

> **Mature Christian:** "*The American Heritage Dictionary of the English Language* (1992) defines fornication as 'Sexual intercourse between partners who are not married to each other.' Does this answer your question?"

So, in what way did our "mature" Christian mishandle the issue? Answer: He selected the wrong dictionary. If we had a dictionary that was published in England at the same time the KJV Bible was published, would we find the definition of the word "fornication" the same as in *The American Heritage Dictionary of the English Language*, published in 1992? No, of course not.

However, we do not even have to go that far back in time, nor do we have to go to England. Let's look at an American dictionary as recent as the 1960's. The *Webster's Seventh New Collegiate Dictionary* (1965) defines fornication as:

> Human sexual intercourse other than between a man and his wife: *sexual intercourse between a spouse and an unmarried person*: sexual intercourse between unmarried people—used in some translations (as AV, DV) of the Bible (as in Mt 5:32) for unchastity (as in RSV) or immorality (as in NCE) to cover all sexual intercourse except between husband and wife or concubine (emphasis mine).[6]

What exactly do we now call "sexual intercourse between a spouse and an unmarried person"? It is called adultery. You see, the word fornication was not limited to only one idea, i.e., sex between unmarried people. It certainly included that as one of its uses, but it was not limited to that. So even as recent as 1965 in America, the word fornication was used for (1) sexual intercourse between a spouse and an unmarried person, which is also called adultery, and (2) sexual intercourse between unmarried people.

The English word *fornication* came from the Latin word *fornix,* which meant "arch." The term was used in reference to a vaulted cellar or similar place where prostitutes plied their trade. It turns out that Roman prostitutes would hang out under the archways of certain public buildings. Prostitution consequently came to be called "going under the arches" or, in a single word, *fornication.* Roman street prostitutes would also hang out underneath the arches of the famed Roman Colosseum. There were also vaulted (arched) cellars where men would go to be with prostitutes.

It appears that the first recorded use of the word *fornication* was in Middle English in the early 14th century, and it had this idea of prostitution in mind. If a man, married or not, had sexual relations with a prostitute, they were both committing fornication, i.e., sexual immorality. And, when a

---

[6] *Webster's Seventh New Collegiate Dictionary*, executive ed. Philip B. Gove, s.v. "fornication," (Springfield, MA: G. & C. Merriam Company, 1965), p. 329.

married man was with a prostitute, this was adultery. Thus, at the time the KJV was translated, the word *fornication* meant any kind of sexual immorality, including adultery, and it was also used in regard to prostitution. In fact, four hundred years ago in merry old England, the English word *fornication* meant any sort of actual sexual misconduct. The definition of fornication as sex between only unmarried people is rather a recent definition and should not be read back into the Bible.

Fornication Breaks the Marriage Covenant in the Old Testament and in the New Testament

So, why did Jesus allow one to initiate a divorce for *fornication?* The believer is not bound to the marriage covenant because his/her spouse has *already broken* that covenant through *fornication* (adultery). Remember that under the Old Testament law, the penalty for adultery was death. The death of the spouse did not break the marriage covenant. Death was the penalty for having broken the marriage covenant through the act of adultery. Today, we do not put people to death for breaking a marriage covenant by an act of adultery. But the marriage covenant is still just as broken as it was in Old Testament times. Thus, the Christian is permitted to divorce his/her spouse because the unfaithful spouse has already broken the marriage covenant, and he/she is "dead" to the spouse.

One caveat here: One must be careful not to see in the words of Jesus a *command* to divorce as the Pharisees saw a *command* to divorce in Moses' allowance to divorce (cf. Matthew 19:7; Deuteronomy 24:1-4). Jesus was not commanding the Christian to divorce the unfaithful spouse. He was only allowing it. So, if one divorces his/her spouse due to fornication (adultery), he/she is not sinning. But the whole message of the gospel is that a person can be forgiven of his or her sins if there is true repentance on the part of the sinner. Thus, it is better, *if possible,* for the innocent spouse to forgive the repentant spouse if he/she is truly repentant. But, please understand that the innocent spouse is under *no biblical obligation* to remain married to the adulterer. So, just as a person is not required to divorce an unfaithful spouse, neither is the person required to stay married to the unfaithful spouse, even if there has been true repentance. It seems apparent that the highest *ideal* and will of God is that there be repentance, forgiveness, and reconciliation between the couple, just as God ultimately did with Israel:

> Go, proclaim this message toward the north: Return, faithless Israel, declares the LORD, I will frown on you no longer, for I am merciful, declares the LORD, I will not be angry forever. Only acknowledge your guilt—you have rebelled against the LORD your God, you have scattered your favors to foreign gods under every spreading tree, and have not obeyed me, declares the LORD (Jeremiah 3: 12-13).

Fornication is Adultery, Incest, and Homosexuality

In the e-mail (mentioned above) that the man sent to me, he stated, "The Bible uses the word *fornication only* in times when it refers to two people, *neither of whom are married* who have sex. It *never* refers to adultery as fornication." However, this is simply not true.

While I believe that this gentleman thought that his desire-belief was true, it wasn't. In fact, his desire-belief blinded him from looking more closely at the Bible, even in the *King James Version*. It is a simple thing to drag out a concordance and look up various passages where the word *fornication* is used and see how it is used elsewhere in Scripture in the KJV.

Sex With His Father's Wife

Interestingly, in First Corinthians, chapter 5, there is an account of a man who was having sexual relations with his father's *wife*. The word that the *King James Version* translation uses for these sexual relations with a married woman is *fornication*.

It is reported commonly that there is *fornication* among

you, and such *fornication* as is not so much as named among the Gentiles, that one should have his father's *wife* (emphasis mine, 1 Corinthians 5:1, KJV).

If we use the narrow, modern-day definition of the word *fornication* and attempt to read it back into 1 Corinthians 5:1, this passage would not make sense. If the e-mail writer were correct, and "The Bible uses the word *fornication only* in times when it refers to two people, *neither of whom are married* who have sex," then apparently this *wife* was not a married woman. However, the term "wife" by definition means a married woman. And, the KJV Bible identifies this wife's adulterous sexual relations with a man who was not her husband as fornication. The Greek word employed for this sexual adultery is *porneia* which is translated as *fornication* in the *King James* translation. This is the same Greek word as in Matthew 5:32 and 19:9 which is also translated *fornication* in the *King James* translation.

Some assume that this woman was his stepmother, and if so, then the fornication taking place was simple adultery. If, however, this woman was actually his biological mother, then the fornication was adultery-incest. In either case, the idea that the KJV Bible only uses the word fornication when it refers to two unmarried people having sex is simply not true. This man was having sex with another man's wife. Thus, she was married, and the *King James* translation calls this adulterous act *fornication*.

Homosexuality

Next, in Jude, verse 7, the writer speaks of the *fornication* of Sodom and Gomorrah. The sexual sin of these people was homosexuality. "Even as Sodom and Gomorrah, and the cities about them in like manner, giving themselves over to fornication, and going after strange flesh, are set forth for an example, suffering the vengeance of eternal fire" (Jude 7, KJV). The term *fornication* in the KJV in the New Testament is used for sexual immorality of almost any kind.

The word *fornication* in the *King James* translation takes into scope illicit sexual relations between any persons whether single or married. Therefore, according to Jesus, marital unfaithfulness is grounds for divorce (Matthew 5:32 and 19:9), and the Christian has permission to initiate the divorce if his/her spouse has been unfaithful to the marriage covenant by committing adultery.

Jesus Never Used The Word Fornication

Not only is it a semantic anachronism to read our modern-day definition of the word *fornication* back into the Bible, but we must also recognize that Jesus never said the word *fornication* in the first place.

The word *fornication* is an English word, and the English language did not develop until centuries after the time of Christ. Jesus probably spoke Aramaic, and Matthew wrote His sayings in Greek. The word that Matthew used to signify what Jesus was referring to in His exception clause was the Greek word *porneia.* In the New Testament, *porneia* is used of illicit sexual relations which includes adultery.

I was once teaching a class on divorce and remarriage and someone made the same comment as the person (mentioned earlier) did in his e-mail. In brief, the person said, *"Jesus said that divorce was only legal for fornication, and that's sex between unmarried people. So, it doesn't refer to adultery."* I think all the people in the class nearly fell out of their chairs when I said, "Guess what. Jesus never used the word *fornication*."

You see, Jesus was not speaking in English, and the *Greek New Testament* never used the word *fornication* at all. It used the word *porneia.* Please understand that the *King James Version* of the New Testament is an English *translation* of the Greek New Testament, and the English usage in the KJV is four hundred years old. Furthermore, not only is the word *fornication* an English word, but when it was placed in the KJV translation, it had a much broader meaning than it does today. Even the *New King James Version* updates the English term to better reflect the Greek word *porneia.* The *New King*

James Version has it as "sexual immorality" (Matthew 5:32; 19:9).

This common misunderstanding that fornication means *sex between unmarried people* occurs when one applies a late 20th and early 21st century definition anachronistically to the Bible. This is a common problem with understanding the English word *fornication*.

So, what's the answer? Simple: First, we must take the time to look at the history of the English word fornication and find out what it meant to the KJV translators four hundred years ago, and we must look at how this word is used in other passages, like 1 Corinthians 5 where even the KJV Bible *clearly* uses the word to mean adultery. Second, we must research what these New Testament passages actually say in the Greek (i.e., *porneia*). And, finally, we must then do research to find out what that Greek term *porneia* actually meant in its New Testament context. When we do these things, we find that the Greek word *porneia* (from which we get our word pornography), which is translated as fornication in the KJV Bible, means any physical, sexual misconduct, *including adultery*.

The King James Bible and a Modern-day Dictionary

An entire argument or theology based solely upon a modern-day understanding of the English word *fornication* is simply irresponsible. After looking at the evidence of the word *fornication*—even in the KJV!—it can be nothing more than a desire-belief that keeps people locked into the *sex-between-unmarried-people* argument.

I often tell young Bible students that one of the worst things that they can do is study their *King James Version* Bibles with a modern-day dictionary as their lexicon. Used in new situations and new contexts, words change meanings.

One of the most obvious word changes in modern English is the word "gay." As late as the mid-1960's the word *gay* meant "Happily excited: merry,"[7] "cheerful," and "lighthearted excitement." If one was gay, he was merry and happy. Some readers may remember the cartoon show *The Flintstones*. Hanna-Barbera produced 30-minute episodes of *The Flintstones* for six seasons (September 30, 1960 to September 2, 1966). In the theme song, the word "gay" is used in its old sense of being "happy" and "cheerful." The closing line says, "We'll have a gay, old time!"[8]

Of course, that is not how this word is used today. In fact, in our culture, the word gay took an entirely new meaning sometime in the 1980's.

Now, we do not read our modern definition back into *The Flintstones* theme song. Perhaps a comedian might do that to get a few laughs, but to do so and really think that's what the theme song meant is to commit the fallacy of semantic anachronism. So, if a word can change so drastically in a mere 20 years within a single culture, how much more can a word (*fornication*) change over a period of four hundred years and in multiple cultures?

Spiritual Adultery

It is also very interesting that the KJV uses the word *fornication* to indicate the idolatries of Israel (and Jerusalem) against the Lord (see, for example, Ezekiel 16, esp. vv. 15-29, and 2 Chronicles 21:11, KJV). However, it should be kept in mind that God says He is *married* to Israel and that she is his *wife*. In fact, in Jeremiah, God gives her a certificate of divorce for her spiritual *adultery*.

---

[7] *Webster's Seventh New Collegiate Dictionary*, executive ed. Philip B. Gove, s.v. "gay," (Springfield, MA: G. & C. Merriam Company, 1965), p. 346.

[8] "Meet The Flintstones": The final few lines of the lyrics say: "When you're, with the Flintstones; Have a yabba, dabba, doo time; A dabba doo time; We'll have a gay, old time!"

If the King James Version was really attempting to signify that fornication was sex between *unmarried* people, why does it use that *very* word to indicate spiritual *adultery*? Should not it be "spiritual sex between unmarried people"? In other words, God does not call the *heathen's* worship of false gods fornication. Rather, He calls His *wife's* worship of false gods fornication; this indicates that she was married to God and committed a spiritual *adultery* (fornication) against Him, and for that, He divorced her.

Concluding Remarks

Remember, it is one thing for you to desire that something be true; it is quite another to act on your desire-beliefs as though they were true. And, it is yet another thing entirely to attempt to force others to live according to *your* desire-beliefs. All of our desire-beliefs must bow the knee to Jesus Christ and His teaching. Jesus said that it is lawful to divorce one's spouse for marital infidelity (Matthew 5:32; 19:9). So, Jesus does in fact permit Christians to initiate divorce when there is adultery on the part of the other spouse.

Study Questions For

Chapter 6
Jesus on Divorce

1. Explain what desire-beliefs are, and what is the author's point concerning desire-beliefs with regard to one's theology about divorce and remarriage?
2. Is it likely that we all have some desire-beliefs? Why or why not?
3. What does the author say is a persistent desire-belief with regard to Jesus and divorce?
4. Define the word *fornication* as it is generally understood today (i.e., in our modern English).
5. What is a Semantic Anachronism?
6. What are the three old words that the author gives from the KJV, and how do they show that words can change meaning over time?
7. Did the word *fornication* mean the same thing four hundred years ago in England (and in 1965 and before in America) as it means today? If not, what are the differences?
8. What was the penalty for adultery under the Old Testament law?
9. Did the death (as a penalty) of the spouse break the marriage covenant, or was the marriage covenant already broken by the spouse's act of adultery?
10. Does the *King James Bible* ever use the word *fornication* in reference to adultery? Give Scripture.
11. What does the author often tell young Bible students is one of the worst things that they can do? Why does he tell them this?

*Remarriage is undeniable proof that wild-eyed
optimism is alive and well.—Kir Notslaw*

Chapter 7

Remarriage Restrictions

The pastor called his superiors at the local denominational district and said,

> "I'm calling to ask for permission to perform a wedding for a couple who have both been married before."

> "Is either ex-spouse of the two still living?" the district official asked.

> "Yes. Both of the ex-spouses are still living" the minister responded.

> "Then I'm afraid that we cannot grant permission for you to perform the ceremony for them."

> "But, don't you want to know the circumstances under which these two people were divorced?" the minister asked the official.

> "No need" said the official, "it's just policy. Our ministers are not to perform weddings for people who have been married before and who have ex-spouses still living."

> "But, both of the ex-spouses have a train wreck for a

life. The ex-husband was a serial child molester, and he's now in prison" said the minister. "And the ex-wife of the man became a bisexual prostitute. The two who want to be married have lived Christian lives through all of this and attempted to work through these things with their ex-spouses. The man even . . ."

"Listen!" the minister was interrupted, "We don't care about the circumstances under which they were divorced. That's not the issue," said the official. "We care only if the ex-spouse is still living, and since the ex-spouses in question are still living, the answer is no, you cannot perform their wedding. They'll just have to find someone else to do it."

Like the official, there are some who believe that no one should ever get remarried if his or her ex-spouse is still living. It matters not to them why the couple divorced. Remarriage is simply always a "no-no." But, is this position biblical? Answer: Not even close.

Remarriage After the Spouse Has Died

The Scripture is clear concerning the idea of remarriage after one's spouse has died. Simply put, it is permissible: "but if her husband dies, she is free from the law, so that she is not an adulteress, though she is joined to another man" (Romans 7:2b). In fact remarriage in some instances is encouraged by Paul: "Therefore, I want the younger widows to get married, bear children, keep house, and give the enemy no occasion for reproach" (1 Timothy 5:14). It is obvious, then, that remarriage in and of itself is not wrong.

Remarriage After Divorce

"When a man takes a wife . . . and he writes her a certificate of divorce and . . . sends her out from his house, and she leaves . . . and becomes another man's wife" (Deuteronomy 24:1-4).

Interestingly, the passage in Deuteronomy 24 speaks of remarriage in a matter-of-fact style. There is no question in this passage concerning whether or not the divorced woman will (or may) remarry; it is simply assumed that she will. Under Old Testament law, remarriage was not only permitted, it was expected. There is no question or debate concerning remarriage in this passage. Neither is there discouragement from remarriage. This passage sees remarriage as an *inevitability*. There are no restrictions concerning the idea of remarriage thus far. In fact, though the first marriage was an arranged one, the second marriage was one by choice. The woman's second marriage could be for love.

Remarriage Restrictions

Remarriage Restriction # 1: The First Husband
Nevertheless, there are some restrictions on remarriage. As stated previously, the passage in Deuteronomy says that if the divorced woman remarries another man and the second husband dies or divorces her, she cannot get remarried to her first husband.

> . . . and if the later husband turns against her and writes her a certificate of divorce . . . or if the latter husband dies who took her to be his wife, then the former husband who sent her away is not allowed to take her again to be his wife, since she has been defiled (Deuteronomy 24:3-4).

Strangely, there are some people today who teach that if one is divorced and remarried and wants to become right with God, then he/she must divorce the second partner and remarry the first partner. However, there is nothing in Scripture, either Old Testament or New Testament, that would lead one to this idea. In fact, Deuteronomy 24:3-4 says just the opposite!
In the late 1980's there was a couple who were the "marriage gurus" for many confused Christians. This couple

often appeared on Christian TV. They wrote books and held seminars in which they touted their many unbiblical ideas. They taught, "No divorce for any reasons whatsoever, and no remarriage."

However, their inconsistent teachings became apparent when they also taught that if a Christian was remarried, the only way that this person would be right with God was to divorce the second spouse and remarry the first spouse (which is in opposition to Deuteronomy 24:3-4). They even said that if the Christian had children by his/her second marriage, it still didn't matter. The person was still to secure a divorce from the second spouse and remarry the first spouse.

And, what if the first spouse was also remarried? Then both of them were to divorce their second spouses and remarry each other.

But what of the other, new spouses? What if this was *their* first marriage? Then, after they were divorced, they themselves could never marry anyone else because that would be a remarriage for them. So, they were to remain single for the rest of their lives. Confused yet?

Some Christian TV programs had this couple teaching their unbiblical and confusing ideas about marriage, divorce, and remarriage. During one question and answer period, a woman asked this couple what she should do. Her husband had divorced her. Now he was remarried, and his new wife was pregnant. The couple told the woman that she was to pray and ask God to make her ex-husband's new wife have a miscarriage! After all, they argued, didn't God take King David's illegitimate baby from Bathsheba?

Wanting to understand the reasoning for their ideas, I bought their book on this topic. I was not surprised to find that neither of them had any formal training in theology or Bible. I wrote them a letter asking for some clarifications about their interpretations of certain passages, and their response letter said, in essence, that God had given them their interpretations and anyone who disagreed with them was simply in rebellion against God.

Where Are They Now?

The following year, this couple was exposed: The woman had actually been married before! Why hadn't she followed her own teaching and divorced her second husband and remarried her first husband? She said it was because it was "different" for her. She never explained how it was different, but she felt that God had given her a "pass" on the very thing that they were telling others to do to be right with God.

Not only that, but they also ended up getting a divorce shortly thereafter. She claimed that her second husband—who sat lovingly holding her hand during their appearances on TV and in their seminars—had been physically abusing her. She confessed that during the time that they were telling others how to conduct their lives on the topics of divorce and remarriage, they themselves were heading for divorce court. Later she appeared on some of the same Christian TV programs and talked about being an abused wife!

In summary, there is no supporting Scripture for the cockeyed idea that if one is divorced and remarried and wants to become right with God, then he/she must leave the second spouse and remarry the first spouse. In fact, just the opposite is true (Deuteronomy 24:1-4).

Does it Apply Today?

Next, is the prohibition of remarrying one's first spouse after having been remarried to someone else still applicable today? While no one should be forced to divorce his/her second spouse and return to his/her first spouse, we must understand the reason *why* Moses imposed this prohibition, and we must ask ourselves if (and how) it applies today. Given the reason why this prohibition from remarrying one's first spouse was put in place to begin with may make this an *ad hoc* situation and not necessarily applicable today.

The reason for this prohibition was because the Israelite men were committing serial divorce and remarriages, and Moses used this prohibition from remarrying one's first spouse as a way to curb this ongoing problem. This particular remarriage restriction protected the woman from a hasty divorce.

So, in our day if Julie divorces Ted and marries another man, but Ted stays single, and then Julie's new husband dies a few years later, is she prohibited from remarrying Ted? Many would say that she is prohibited from remarrying Ted based on Deuteronomy 24:4. However, we must consider the context of the passage both scripturally and culturally. It appears that this passage may not be universally prohibiting a person from remarrying his/her first spouse after that person has been married and then separated from his/her spouse by death or a scripturally sanctioned divorce. It seems wise to prayerfully and thoughtfully consider each case on its own merits rather than arbitrarily apply a scriptural prohibition that likely was never intended to be universally applied. A fascinating passage seems to indicate that God did not lock himself into this rule.

> They say, if a man put away his wife, and she go from him, and become another man's, shall he return unto her again? shall not that land be greatly polluted? but thou hast played the harlot with many lovers; yet return again to me, saith the LORD. . . . Go and proclaim these words toward the north, and say, Return, thou backsliding Israel, saith the LORD; and I will not cause mine anger to fall upon you: for I am merciful, saith the LORD, and I will not keep anger for ever (KJV, Jeremiah 3:1, 12).

Remarriage Restriction # 2 The Priests

Another restriction on remarriage is found in Leviticus 21:7. It states that a priest was forbidden to marry a divorced woman. There were restrictions placed on the leaders of God's people that did not always apply to lay people. "They [the priests] shall not take a woman who is profaned by harlotry, nor shall they take a woman divorced from her husband; for he is holy to his God" (Leviticus 21:7). But, again, does this remarriage restriction have application for today? Shall we assume that today's counterparts to the Leviticus priests are the leaders of the Christian churches? Thus, shall a minister not marry a woman who was formerly a prostitute but who has since repented and become born-again? This prohibition also seems to be culturally bound.

Remarriage Restriction # 3 Without Just Cause

Jesus also forbids the remarriage of persons who have divorced without just cause (Matthew 5:32; 19:9; Mark 10:11-12; Luke 16:18). Omitting the exception clause for the moment, Jesus' words restricting remarriage shall be examined.

> I say to you that everyone who divorces his wife . . . makes her commit adultery; and whoever marries a divorced woman commits adultery (Matthew 5:32).

This passage is not culturally bound nor is it an *ad hoc* response to a singular historical situation. Thus, this passage has universal applicability.

This passage has the woman's remarriage in view. The first husband is guilty of "forcing" her to commit adultery, and the man who marries this divorced woman is also guilty of adultery. In this passage, though the first husband is guilty of causing the woman to commit adultery, it does not speak of his remarriage nor whether it would also be considered adultery. However, another statement of Jesus clears this up quite well:

> And I say to you, whoever divorces his wife . . . and marries another woman commits adultery (Matthew 19:9).

In Mark 10:11-12 Jesus states:

> Whoever divorces his wife and marries another woman commits adultery against her; and if she herself divorces her husband and marries another man, she is committing adultery.

Lastly, in Luke 16:18 Jesus says,

> Everyone who divorces his wife and marries another commits adultery; and he who marries one who is divorced from a husband commits adultery.

Since Jesus cannot condone nor promote adultery, the obvious conclusion is that he was forbidding the remarriage of divorced persons. However, it must be made abundantly clear that this is a remarriage restriction when there is *no just cause* for the divorce to begin with.

Note well that Jesus does not say that a person who is divorced for a justifiable reason (i.e., adultery) commits adultery when he or she remarries. The only time that the remarriage is adultery is when there is no just cause for the initial divorce. Jesus tells us what that "just cause" for divorce is in Matthew 5:32 and 19:9 in what is known as the *exception clause*. The *exception clause* will be discussed more in the next chapter.

Remarriage Restriction # 4 Christian Couples

The apostle Paul also places restrictions on remarriage. Paul states that a Christian couple is not to divorce. However, if they disobey this command, which he attributes to the Lord, then they are to remain single, not remarrying. This leaves open an opportunity and availability for a reconciliation between the divorced Christians (1 Corinthians 7:10-11).

Some Christian couples have wrongly taken the words of Paul *that if an unbeliever decides to leave (divorce) let him/her leave*, to mean that if they do not have the same calling on their lives, they can leave one another. Since they feel like they have a "mixed-faith" situation, they come to feel that they have the apostle's blessing to divorce and each one follow what it is that he or she believes God has called him or her specifically for. Since they feel that they have the blessing of Scripture to divorce, they would also have the same blessing to remarry.

However, when Paul speaks about the unbeliever leaving in 1 Corinthians 7:12-16, he is *not* speaking about the difference of the calling God has placed on Christian individuals, but the difference is in whether the individual is or is not a born-again believer in Jesus Christ. This is fully realized when one looks at Paul's full treatment of the situation. In verses 12-13 he speaks of the "unbelieving" wife and husband. No differences in the calling of God is mentioned, only the difference between the *brother* and an *unbelieving wife*. Then Paul sets up a contrast between the woman (*sister*) and an *unbelieving husband*.

It is true that there can be much turmoil in a situation where the husband and the wife feel that they have been given different callings by God. This sort of situation calls for much prayer and dying to self. In some cases it may call for the couple to seek pastoral or professional counseling. It is not within the scope of this book to give an answer to a situation of that kind. Nevertheless, divorce in this situation is not an option, and it is forbidden by both Jesus and Paul (Mark 10:11-12, 1 Corinthians 7:10). Married believers are not to divorce. If, however, the Christian couple does divorce, they are restricted from remarriage, unless of course they remarry each other.

As noted above, the law, Jesus, and the apostle Paul have put restrictions on remarriage. But are there situations where remarriage is an acceptable option?

Study Questions For

Chapter 7
Remarriage Restrictions

1. Is it permissible for one to remarry after his/her spouse has died? Give Scripture.

2. In Deuteronomy 24:1-4 is there a question or debate concerning remarriage?

3. What restriction on remarriage is stated in Deuteronomy 24:3-4?

4. Some today teach that if one is divorced and remarried and wants to become right with God, then he/she must divorce his/her second partner and remarry the first partner. What does Deuteronomy 24:3-4 say about this?

5. Is there any supporting Scripture for the idea that if one is divorced and remarried and wants to become right with God, then he/she must leave his/her second spouse and remarry the first spouse?

6. Why must we understand the reason that Moses imposed the prohibition of remarrying one's first spouse after having been remarried to someone else?

7. Is Moses' prohibition still applicable today? Why or why not?

8. Why is it that in Leviticus 21:7 a priest was forbidden to marry a divorced woman? And, is this prohibition still applicable today?

9. When does Jesus forbid the remarriage of persons who have divorced?

10. Some see Paul's words that *if an unbeliever decides to divorce let him/her leave* to mean that if a Christian couple does not have the same calling on their lives, they can leave one another. Is this the correct intent of Paul's statement?

*We should be careful to get out of an experience only the
wisdom that is in it and stop there; lest we be like the cat
that sits down on a hot stove-lid. She will never sit down
on a hot stove-lid again and that is well; but also she will
never sit down on a cold one anymore.—Mark Twain*

Chapter 8

Remarriage Options

Is Remarriage Ever an Option?

Bob came into Dr. Kimbel's office and sat down. Dr.
Kimbel had been a pastor for many years but was no longer
pastoring. He had also been a professor of New Testament
theology. But now he was a full-time Christian counselor.

Bob was about 50 years old, but he looked much older.
He seemed tired and unhappy. The counselor began the
session by asking Bob a question.

"Well, Bob, what brings you to see me today?"

Bob just sat there for a moment before he answered,
and then finally, "Well, I'm afraid that I have made a
big mistake."

"You want to tell me about it?" The counselor asked.

Bob inhaled deeply, and spoke softly, "Yeah, but I just
feel that I've wasted so much of my life that it's hard to
even talk about. But, I need to know for sure if I've
made a mistake, or if I was right all along."

Dr. Kimbel sat forward in his chair and leaned in toward Bob. With concern etched in his face he gently said, "You're going to have to be a lot more specific Bob."

"Well see, it's like this" said Bob, "twenty-seven years ago my wife divorced me and ran off with another man. And I know that the apostle Paul says that a Christian couple is not supposed to divorce, but if they do, then they are to remain single and not get remarried. And, Jesus also says that being remarried is a sin."

Not knowing quite where Bob was going yet, Dr. Kimbel asked, "Ok. So, what does this have to do why you're here to see me today?"

"Well, Doc, just this past week I was listening to a radio preacher, and he said that remarriage isn't sin if the reason you are divorced is because your wife committed adultery and had an affair with another man."

"That's true," said Dr. Kimbel.

"So, then," Bob went on, "I've stayed single for the last 27 years because of something I believed in that doesn't even exist?"

"What do you mean?" asked Dr. Kimbel.

"Well, Doc, the only reason I stayed single for the last twenty-seven years was because I thought I was being holy and good by not getting remarried. I figured if I got remarried, I'd be committing adultery, but if you can get remarried without it being sin because your wife had an affair, then I've been believing in the wrong thing, and I just wasted the last 27 years of my life."

"Oh, I see," said Dr. Kimbel. "So, the only reason why you never remarried is because you thought that if you did, you'd be living in sin?"

"Exactly!" said Bob. "That's what my pastor back then told me, and I believed him."

"Well, Bob, didn't you ever read for yourself what Jesus said about this?" Dr. Kimbel asked.

"Yeah, sure I did, but my pastor always told me what it meant," Bob responded. "And he said that I was just to pray that God would bring my wife back to me and I was to stay single until she came home. And, if she never did, then I'd be okay anyway because I was following the Bible. And he said that the apostle Paul says that the only remarriage that a Christian couple can have is if they remarry each other. And, since she was married to another man, I couldn't very well remarry her, so I had to stay single."

Bob had invested 27 years of his life in a belief that was derived from a confused understanding of Scripture. Now he was faced with a very difficult crossroad. Would he continue to believe in this confused idea about remarriage so that he could feel justified for having shunned the prospects of remarriage for the last 27 years of his life, or would he face the Scriptures squarely and accept what they clearly state?

Beyond God's Regulations

I was at a ministers' conference some years ago. Over lunch with about eight other men and women in ministry, the topic of divorce and remarriage came up. One woman at the table was very outspoken about her views. It was the same one that Bob had held for 27 years. She was adamant that there should be no remarriage unless the ex-spouse was dead. When I asked her to specifically address the exception clause found in Matthew 5:32 and in Matthew 19:9, she said:

First of all, the so-called exception clause is only found in Matthew. It's not in Mark or Luke or John. So, that's three against one. Next, even if the exception clause is real, it is better to be holy than to take the easy way out and use the exception clause.[9]

As illogical as this statement was—and it was wrong on so many levels—I was even more stunned when I saw and heard several of the ministers at the table nodding their heads in agreement and saying "amen" between bites of food.

So I asked her if salvation by faith alone was the "easy way out" and if she thought that we should add some works to our salvation. Of course she responded in the negative and said that works doesn't save anyone and that we are saved by faith alone.

I agreed with her answer, but then I asked why it was that she followed God's Word on the issue of salvation but not on the issue of remarriage? I told her that she was saying that it was "holy" to go beyond God's regulations. That somehow, God didn't go "far enough" on this issue, so she was helping Him out by adding something that He never stated: i.e., *no remarriage for any reason other than death of the ex-spouse.* And, this "adding to" God's laws is what is called "legalism" and "self-righteousness," not holiness.

It is self-destructive to impose legalism upon oneself, but it ranks in the category of sin for a Christian leader to impose legalism upon others. So, the real sin was not with the person who remarried on scriptural grounds but with the Christian leader who imposes rules and regulations that go beyond God's rules and regulations.

---

[9] As stated elsewhere, Christians are not to accept one passage at the exclusion (or ignoring) of another; rather, we are to harmonize passages to discover a fuller picture. This woman, however, went far beyond simply accepting one passage while ignoring others. She actually pitted Matthew's account of Christ's words against those of Mark, Luke, and John. A more grievous assault on proper hermeneutics would be difficult to find.

The Exception Clause

In the midst of Jesus' statements about husbands unlawfully divorcing their wives and causing them to commit adultery, and they themselves also committing adultery should they remarry, comes what is known as the *exception clause.*

Jesus speaks of many things in His discourse referred to as the Sermon on the Mount (Matthew 5-7), two of which are divorce and remarriage. He says, "everyone who divorces his wife, except for the cause of unchastity, makes her commit adultery" (Matthew 5:32). When the woman is guilty of adultery, divorcing her does not make her commit adultery; she is already guilty of that sin. When the woman has already committed adultery, the man is free from the marriage covenant which the woman has already broken because of her adultery.

It is important to note that Jesus was dealing with believers (i.e., Jews). Jesus was not dealing with the mixed-marriage (believers with unbelievers) situation here. And it is to believers that Jesus states that there is one, and only one, legitimate reason for divorce: marital unfaithfulness. Matthew 19 also gives the exception clause. "I tell you that anyone who divorces his wife, except for marital unfaithfulness, and marries another woman commits adultery" (Matthew 19:9).

Some argue that these exception clauses should not be given heed because the other Synoptic Gospels do not record them (nor does John). However, rather than arguing for a position because something is not there, it seems much more logical and exegetical to argue for something that is there. The other gospels do not record the exception clause, yet Matthew records it, and he does so twice (Matthew 5:32 and 19:9). Biblical scholars and Bible-believing Christians in all generations have accepted the historicity of the exception clause. Matthew 5:32 and 19:9 are holy Scripture and demand our attention and allegiance, not rejection. Contrary to some ill-conceived, popular ideas, we cannot pick and choose which Scriptures we will accept or reject. As Christians, we are obligated to accept the entire Bible as our sole guide for faith and practice.

Extent of Exception Clauses

Next, we need to determine how far these exception clauses extend. Do the exception clauses refer only to the divorce aspect of the passage, or do they refer to the remarriage aspect as well?

In Matthew 19:9, Jesus says if a man remarries after divorcing his wife (unless he divorced her for fornication) he commits adultery. The final point of this passage is the person's standing within the context of his new marriage. The custom of the people of Jesus' time was one of divorce *and* remarriage.

Remarriage was the rule not the exception. So when Jesus answered the Pharisees' question, he naturally had in mind the social climate of his day.

There is no way of separating divorce and remarriage in Matthew 5:32 and 19:9. *The whole point* of the statement about adultery is pointing us to the second marriage. It is obvious that in the cultural milieu of his day, Jesus assumes the man (Matthew 19:9) and the woman (Matthew 5:32) will remarry. The exception clause deals with divorce *and remarriage*, not just one or the other.

Some point out that Romans 7 makes no exception to the dissolution of marriage by death alone. Some have attempted to use this as "proof" that there is no other reason for a marriage to be broken. However, as stated elsewhere, one passage cannot be accepted to the exclusion of another. Since Romans 7 states that marriage is dissolved by death, then death does indeed dissolve the marriage covenant. But also, since Matthew 5:32 and 19:9 state that adultery dissolves the marriage, then adultery also breaks the marriage covenant. It is not an either/or interpretation but rather a both/and: *both* death *and* adultery break the marriage covenant.

There is no doubt that the exception clauses extend to remarriage. Therefore, when one divorces a spouse on the grounds of adultery, it is simply a recognition of the fact that the marriage covenant *has already been broken by the adulterer*, and the innocent party has the scriptural option to divorce and remarry.

Paul's Exception

Though Paul gives no exception for remarriage other than death in Romans 7, he does give an exception in 1 Corinthians 7:15. In this exception Paul is dealing with mixed-marriages (believers married to unbelievers). Paul says, "Yet if the unbelieving one leaves, let him leave. The brother or sister is not under bondage [not enslaved] in such cases, but God has called us to peace." Paul says that the remaining believer is "not under bondage in such cases." The word bondage (*douloo*) means "to enslave" or "bring into (or be under) bondage."

The term "not under bondage" has definite implications for the innocent party. Those implications find their root in the often asked question: Is the person only free from an unsaved spouse, or is he/she free to actually remarry someone else?

As noted above, the term bondage (*douloo*) means to make one a slave. In Old Testament times among the Hebrews, a person who was in debt beyond his ability to pay his bills could sell or hire himself out to servanthood (Leviticus 25:39). In this setting, however, a relative of the slave could redeem him from slavery at any time (Leviticus 25:48-49). If no one bought him out of slavery, his master would set him free after six years of service (Deuteronomy 15:12-14). When a slave was set free, either by the redemption payment of a relative or at the end of six years of service, he was a completely free man. In fact he was freed from his previous master to the extent that he could voluntarily become the slave of a different master. He was no longer "under bondage" to his first master. This is the same idea in Paul's words when he says, "The brother or sister is not under bondage in such cases" (1 Corinthians 7:15b). Paul does not say the remaining believer is not free to remarry as he does in verse 11 when speaking of Christians divorcing. So, while a Christian should not initiate the divorce, Paul states that when the unbeliever initiates the divorce, the believer is "not under bondage" to that relationship, and the implication is that he or she is free to resubmit himself/herself to a new partner. Thus, the person who has been divorced by the nonbeliever is free from the marriage covenant and, thus, free to remarry.

Remarriage, however, may not always be in the best interest of the divorcé. Note here that Paul says,

> Are you bound to a wife? Do not seek to be released. Are you released from a wife? Do not seek a wife. . . . But I want you to be free from concern. One who is unmarried is concerned about the things of the Lord, how he may please the Lord; but one who is married is concerned about the things of the world, how he may please his wife, and his interests are divided (NASB, 1 Corinthians 7:27, 32-34a).

Though Paul does discourage remarriage here, he does not say that it is against the will of God. In 1 Corinthians 7:27, Paul says, "Are you bound to a wife? Do not seek to be released. Are you released from a wife? Do not seek a wife." The word *released* is used twice in this verse. It is the same Greek word (or inflection of the same word) each time translated as *released* (or *loosed* as in the *King James Version*).

Let's look at the NASB and the KJV on this verse:

Are you bound to a wife? Do not seek to be **released**. Are you **released** from a wife? Do not seek a wife (NASB, 1 Corinthians 7:27).

Art thou bound unto a wife? seek not to be **loosed**. Art thou **loosed** from a wife? seek not a wife (KJV, 1 Corinthians 7:27).

Note that the key word is repeated twice (and I have placed them in bold). Again, this is the same Greek word, so it is proper that it would be repeated in English as the same word each time, and the NASB and the KJV do a good job of doing so. So, what does the Greek word translated as **released** in the

NASB and as **loosed** in the KJV mean? W. E. Vine says that it means *divorced.*[10]

Interestingly, the *New International Version* helps us a little here on this passage when it translates it this way:

> Are you married? Do not seek a **divorce**. Are you **unmarried**? Do not look for a wife (emphasis mine, 1 Corinthians 7:27).

I say that the the *New International Version* helps us a little because while it correctly updates the Greek word in question to divorce (as W. E. Vine says it is), it is not consistent in doing so. The second time the word is used, the NIV translates it as *unmarried*. The inconsistency here is what often creates a misunderstanding. Since the Greek word *released* (or *loosed* as in the *King James Version*) is the same word used twice, why not translate it into English the same way twice? Thus, it could say,

> Are you married? Do not seek a **divorce**. Are you **divorced**? Do not look for a wife (emphasis mine, 1 Corinthians 7:27).

But, note, however, the first part of the next verse. It says, "But if you do marry, you have not sinned" (1 Corinthians 7:28a). When verses 27 and 28a are read together it says:

> Are you married? Do not seek a divorce. Are you divorced? Do not look for a wife. But if you do marry, you have not sinned (1 Corinthians 7:27-28a).

Therefore, if a person is divorced on scriptural grounds and then remarries, he/she has not sinned.

[10] W. E. Vine, Merrill F. Unger, and William White Jr., *Vine's Complete Expository Dictionary of Old and New Testament Words* (Nashville, TN: Thomas Nelson Publishers, 1985), p. 379.

It is quite clear from this passage of Scripture that remarriage is not the "unpardonable" sin. Paul says, are you divorced? Then don't go looking for a spouse, *but if you do remarry, you have not sinned.*

That Paul is speaking to divorced persons here rather than just people who have never been married needs to be established. Paul himself clears up to whom he is speaking in verse 28 after he says, "But if you do marry, you have not sinned," by going on to say, "and if a virgin should marry, she has not sinned." Now obviously a virgin is one who has never been married. The reason Paul makes the distinction of speaking specifically of the virgin is because he had been addressing divorcés (the *released*, or *loosed*), and not simply the *unmarried*, but then he shifts his address to the virgin (*unmarried*). So there are clearly two different groups of people in this passage. Those who are *released*, and the *unmarried*: the *divorced* and the *virgin*.

Remarriage—A New Covenant

The issue has already been settled that if a person is divorced on scriptural grounds and then remarries, the new marriage that is entered into is not an adulterous one.

However, when a person gets a divorce and remarries but has no scriptural grounds for doing so, he/she is clearly committing an act of adultery (Matthew 5:32; 19:9; Mark 10:11-12; Luke 16:18).

And, what if a person has been divorced and remarried without scriptural grounds and then wants to become a Christian, what is this person to do? Is this person to divorce the second spouse and return to the first? Or is this person to stay in the new, second marriage?

Some teach the erroneous idea that if people are divorced and remarried without proper scriptural justification, then they are living in a state of continual adultery. If such a person wishes to become right with God, he/she must divorce the second spouse and remarry the original mate.

What often leads to the misguided teaching that the person must break off the second marriage and remarry the former partner is the idea that the second marriage has been nothing more than a continual state of adultery. According to Jesus when one remarries after divorcing unlawfully, there is definitely adultery as a result. But it appears that there is no such thing as a state of adultery.[11]

Adultery is an act; it is not a continuing state. So, within the new marriage there is the sin of adultery, and this is a sin against the previous marriage covenant. But at that point, the first covenant is then broken and the second covenant entered into. Since the first covenant is broken, the former partner is also now free to remarry. Since the second covenant has been entered into, it is incumbent upon the couple of the new marriage to be faithful to it. In fact, God expects the new covenant—even when entered into inappropriately—to be honored by all parties.

A Scriptural Example

In the book of Joshua, the Gibeonites tricked Joshua and the leaders of Israel into thinking that they were from a distant land. Israel was at war with their close neighbors, and God was giving them victory over their enemies. "However, when the people of Gibeon heard what Joshua had done to Jericho and Ai, they resorted to a ruse: They went as a delegation whose donkeys were loaded with worn-out sacks and old wineskins, cracked and mended. The men put worn and patched sandals on their feet and wore old clothes. All the bread of their food supply was dry and moldy.

Then they went to Joshua in the camp at Gilgal and said to him and the men of Israel, 'We have come from a distant country; make a treaty with us'" (Josh. 9:3-6).

---

[11] Carroll D. Osburn, "The Present Indicative in Matthew 19:9," *Restoration Quarterly*, Volume 24/Number 4. In this article, Osburn says basically this: while the word adultery *moichatai* is in the present tense, that does not settle the issue; context, more than simple tense (or aspect), determines if it is continuous or not. <http://www.restorationquarterly. org/Volume_024/rq02404osburn.htm> (15 August 2005).

Joshua and his men "sampled their provisions but did not inquire of the LORD" (Josh. 9:14). "Then Joshua made a treaty of peace with them to let them live, and the leaders of the assembly ratified it by oath.

Three days after they made the treaty with the Gibeonites, the Israelites heard that they were neighbors, living near them. So the Israelites set out and on the third day came to their cities: Gibeon, Kephirah, Beeroth and Kiriath Jearim. But the Israelites did not attack them, because the leaders of the assembly had sworn an oath to them by the LORD, the God of Israel.

The whole assembly grumbled against the leaders, but all the leaders answered, 'We have given them our oath by the LORD, the God of Israel, and we cannot touch them now'" (Josh. 9:15-19).

So, the Bible indicates that God expects contracts to be kept even when entered into wrongly. Likewise, the new, second marriage is to be honored, and there is to be no divorcing and returning to the former spouse. God recognizes the new marriage as a lawful covenant, and the married partners are to be faithful to that covenant and to God.

Study Questions For

Chapter 8
Remarriage Options

1. What does the author say about self-imposed legalism and legalism imposed upon others?
2. Is it possible for a Christian leader to impose rules and regulations that go beyond God's rules and regulations?
3. In what passages do we find what is known as the exception clause?
4. Who gave the exception clause?
5. Who has accepted the historicity of the exception clause?
6. Does the exception clause refer only to the divorce aspect of the passage, or does it refer to the remarriage aspect as well?
7. Since Romans 7 makes no exception to the dissolution of marriage by death alone, is this proof that there is no other reason for a marriage to be broken?
8. In Paul's exception in 1 Corinthians 7:15, what kind of marriage is Paul dealing with?
9. If a person gets a divorce on scriptural grounds, is it a sin if he/she remarries?
10. If a person gets a divorce and remarries but has no scriptural grounds for doing so, is he/she committing an act of adultery?
11. Is there such a thing as a state of adultery? Why or why not?
12. How does the author use the story of when the Gibeonites tricked Joshua and the leaders of Israel in relation to a second marriage which is predicated upon a divorce with no scriptural justification?

To bear with patience wrongs done to oneself is a mark of perfection, but to bear with patience wrongs done to someone else is a mark of imperfection and even of actual sin.—Thomas Aquinas

Chapter 9

An Unrepentant Continual State of Adultery

Hardhearted Betty

The woman was shunned by nearly the entire congregation. The pastor had told those in leadership that Betty was in sin because she was filing for divorce from her husband, and word had spread fast. Now even Polly Pewsitter was in on the gossip.

Betty's husband, Jasper, had the sympathies of nearly everyone in the church. Jasper had been in the pastor's office on many occasions and with tears streaming down his face, he pleaded with the pastor to help him straighten Betty out. The pastor gave it his best shot.

Betty had been in counseling with the pastor for months but to no avail. She would not change her heart. It was, sadly, set. So, since Betty had no change of heart and since her husband was so hurt, nearly everyone in the church felt like Betty was the "bad guy" and her husband, Jasper, was the injured party.

What had happened to make Betty so hardhearted? Jasper had multiple affairs with both prostitutes and women he had picked up in bars. Jasper had even been physically abusive to Betty. So why was the entire congregation upset at Betty and so welcoming to Jasper?

Betty had known for some time that Jasper was having multiple affairs. They lived in a small town and everyone seemed to know everyone else, or at least they knew someone who knew everyone else. Soon, Betty was informed by more than one "concerned" person about Jasper's dalliances.

Betty confronted Jasper who made no effort to hide his indiscretions. He openly admitted to the multiple affairs. But it didn't stop, and sometimes he'd even stay out all night. On one occasion he actually brought one of his "girlfriends" home while he grabbed a change of clothes and ran out. Betty was subjected to the most degrading humiliation as she tried to maintain a normal home life for her two children.

After a few months of pleading with Jasper and praying for him nearly night and day, she went to their pastor and told him everything that was going on. She told the pastor that her heart was broken beyond repair and that she also worried that Jasper may have contracted a sexually transmitted disease. She asked the pastor if she had grounds to divorce Jasper. The pastor said, "Only if he doesn't repent."

The pastor called Jasper and requested that he come into his office. Once there, Jasper broke down, started crying, and apologized for his multiple affairs.

The pastor then told Betty that she had no grounds for divorce because Jasper had repented. Believing that her pastor knew the Bible well, she did not file for a divorce. For the next three months Jasper was the model husband. He was in church with Betty every Wednesday night and twice on Sundays. Then, without warning, Jasper didn't come home after work one Friday. He was back to his cheating ways. She struggled to hold her life together for the next few months, and she prayed more earnestly than ever before. She begged him to come home and be a father to their children, but nothing worked. Embarrassed and humiliated, once again she talked to their pastor; once again the pastor confronted Jasper; once again he repented with tears, and once again the pastor told Betty that she had no grounds for divorce because Jasper had repented.

This whole sad scenario played itself out for yet a third time ending with the pastor once again telling Betty that she had no grounds to divorce Jasper. This time, however, she filed for a divorce.

Soon the church was abuzz with the gossip that this hardhearted woman was "in sin" because she had filed for a divorce from her husband without scriptural grounds. In the meantime, Jasper came to church every time the doors were open, cried throughout the services, and moped around as though he were a beaten man. Some of the other ladies in the church started feeling sorry for poor Jasper. "That hardhearted Betty," they would say, "how can she treat him this way?"

How Many Adulteries to be Stoned?

As has already been determined the word fornication (*porneia*) denotes a wide variety of sexual activity including premarital, extramarital, homosexual, incestuous, and so on.

However, some (like Betty's pastor) argue that the word fornication (*porneia*) in the exception clause is not referring to a single act of adultery, but it is referring to an ongoing, unrepentant sexual affair. After all, some argue, fornication (*porneia*) is used in Scripture to indicate an illicit relationship or lifestyle. Paul uses the word *porneia* in 1 Corinthians when he rebukes the Corinthian church for allowing fornication of great perversion *to go on* in their midst without putting a stop to it (1 Corinthians 5:1-2). Jude 7 speaks of the fornication of the wicked cities of Sodom, Gomorrah, and the surrounding cities. God destroyed those cities because of their *continual* fornication.

This idea of demanding that *porneia* be a "continual state of adultery" has some disturbing consequences in real life. The story of Betty and Jasper is, sadly, a true story. And, how did the pastor and the church come to such a skewed idea that made Betty out to be the "bad guy" and saw Jasper as the offended party? Their faulty perspective came directly from the idea that the word *porneia* in the exception clause is not referring to a single act of adultery but rather to the unrepentant continuation of an illicit sexual affair.

However, there is nothing in the word *porneia* itself that denotes a "state of continuation." There is no semantic reason for that assumption. Next, there is nothing in the contexts where the word appears that demands that the word has to have the connotation of continuation.

Certainly *porneia* can be an ongoing sin, but so can any sin. However, one act of adultery is *porneia* just as one act of thievery is stealing. Just as it takes only one act of thievery to be a thief, it takes only one act of *porneia* to be an adulterer.

Also, note the breakdown of logic if we assign the continuation idea to the word: if a man commits a single act of adultery (*porneia*) and then repents, he would not have committed adultery (*porneia*) at all because according to their argument, *porneia* only exits when it is in a continual state. If a person commits a single act of homosexuality (*porneia*) and then repents, he would not have committed *porneia* at all because according to their argument, *porneia* only exists in its continual state. The list could go on and on. It is absurd to suggest that a continual state must be in effect for *porneia* to be *porneia*. It is wrong semantically; it is wrong contextually; it is wrong logically.

Our Theology Has Consequences

I am certainly not suggesting that a person must divorce his or her spouse if the person has been unfaithful one time. I am suggesting, however, that we not read into the word *porneia* some continual state of unrepentant sexual immorality when it is not there. Bad theology often has bad consequences. Sometimes those bad consequences affect the lives of innocent people, like Betty and her children.

Instead of her pastor and her church standing behind her as they should have, their faulty theology made them turn the entire situation upside down, and Betty was made to feel like the one who broke her marriage covenant. In reality, however, it was her manipulative and adulterous husband who had broken the marriage covenant. He had broken the marriage covenant by selfishly committing adultery on multiple occasions, and he had done so with utter disregard for his wife and for their children.

Study Questions For

Chapter 9
An Unrepentant Continual State of Adultery

1. Some maintain that the word *porneia* in the exception clause is not referring to a single act of adultery but rather the continuation of an illicit sexual affair. Do you agree? Why or why not?

2. The author says that this idea of a "continual state of adultery" has some disturbing consequences in real life. Why does he say this?

3. Does the word *porneia* itself denote a "state of continuation"?

4. How does the author show that there is a breakdown of logic if we assign the continuation connotation to the word *porneia*?

5. How many times did people have to commit adultery under the Old Testament law before they were put to death by stoning?

*A theoretical faith that takes no account of
practical affairs and does not help to solve them
is no faith at all.—Theme of the Epistle of James*

Chapter 10

Pastoral Practicalities
Counseling People With Regard to
Divorce and Remarriage

John was a young pastor of a local church. A couple in his church was having marital problems, and they went to him for counsel. Knowing that I had dealt with these issues many times as a pastor and counselor and that I had written a book on divorce and remarriage,[12] he approached me and asked what I thought about this couple's situation.

Eric and Janna

Eric and Janna had been married for seven years. They had no children. Janna left Eric and got an apartment of her own. Neither Eric nor Janna had committed adultery, and both of them continued to attend the church. Eric didn't want a divorce, but Janna did. Not long after she moved out, Janna was offered a job out of town, and she took it. When confronted by her pastor, Janna told him that she simply wasn't happy being married. She said that her new job made her happy, and she wanted to devote her time and energy to her career.

---

[12] Walston, *Divorce and Remarriage* (Gospel Publishing House, 1991).

A Necessary Digression

I must digress here and make some points about happiness: Marriage is not an institution created by God to make humans happy. In fact, I know of no married couple who have always been happy with each other. So, if people think that marriage will make them happy, all they have to do is talk with a married couple who have been married for more than two years, and they will discover that marriage is not the "magic pill" of happiness. God never promised that marriage would bring happiness. While there are many couples who are happy together, this is always a qualified happiness. In other words, happiness in marriage is possible but not consistently possible. I have met couples who are very happy with their marriage, but it is a relative happiness. Like everything in this life, circumstances, people, things, job promotions, and whatever else bring happiness only for a time. Wait a while, and the newness wears off. After that, happiness is often something that you achieve by hard work. So, while my wife and I are happy with each other, she is not *always* happy with me, nor I with her. But, we do not find our ultimate happiness from each other. We find our happiness in knowing who we are in Christ, and in knowing that one day we will shed this mortality for immortality. In the meantime, we have discovered that to be temporarily happy in this life, we must strive to make the other person happy. The extent to which I make my wife happy, I find happiness in return.

Over the years, I have been blessed to meet some very happy couples, people who after many years of marriage are more in love than ever. People who would die for their spouses without a second thought. And, yet, in spite of this love and self-sacrifice, they are not always happy with each other.

I will resist the temptation to move into the area of psychology and talk about how one achieves and hopefully maintains happiness, but suffice it to say that happiness is best achieved and maintained when one seeks to make others happy. Though this sounds contradictory, Jesus speaks of this same principle when he says, "For whoever wants to save his life will lose it, but whoever loses his life for me will save it"

(Luke 9:24).

However, self-sought happiness is fleeting and the people that bring happiness to us are fleeting as well. Happiness is not an event; it's not a thing, and it's not a person, not even your spouse. Only immature, self-centered people think that their spouses are there to make them happy.

While certain events, things, and people can make you happy, since all of these are fleeting, the happiness they bring will be fleeting as well.

The News is Bleak

So, for Janna who is no longer happy being married to Eric, the news is bleak. She's looking for sustained happiness in all the wrong places. A divorce might make her happy, but that happiness is fleeting. Her new job might make her happy, but that too is fleeting. I have met people who thought that a divorce would make them happy. And, for a while, it did. But, in due time these same people once again found themselves unhappy and looking for their next "happiness fix."

Janna not only left Eric, but she signed divorce papers as well. A couple of months later, Eric found himself in a courtroom hearing a judge announce that Eric and Janna were no longer husband and wife.

He now sat before his pastor and asked, "What am I to do? What are my biblical options? May I date other women? May I remarry? Or, must I remain single?"

Pastor John gave Eric what I consider to be incorrect biblical advice. He told Eric that since Janna had "deserted" him, he was free to date again and even remarry. So, I asked the pastor from where he got this idea of "desertion." He said that Paul had taught this in 1 Corinthians chapter 7:15. This passage says, "But if the unbeliever leaves, let him do so. A believing man or woman is not bound in such circumstances; God has called us to live in peace."

The issues here are at least two, and here is what they are not: First, Paul is not addressing the situation of two married Christians. Second, Paul is not addressing the idea of desertion.

The two issues are these: First, Paul is explicitly addressing the situation of a mixed-marriage. This is a non-Christian married to a Christian (not two married Christians, as Eric and Janna were). Second, Paul is specifically addressing the issue of *allowance* (not the issue of desertion).

He is saying that if the unsaved person desires to divorce his/her Christian spouse, the Christian does not have to attempt to keep the unsaved spouse in the marriage. It may be that this was a question that the Corinthians had asked him. It may have gone something like this:

> Dear Paul, in our community we have some believers who are married to unbelievers. Sometimes the unbelievers wish to divorce their Christian spouses. However, we know that marriage is sacred, so how should the Christian spouses respond to this? Should a Christian spouse do everything in his/her power to keep the non-Christian spouse from leaving?

His answer may seem counterintuitive, but Paul says that the Christian may *let the unsaved person leave* (i.e., divorce).

It appears from the fact that Paul says that the Christian may *allow* the unsaved spouse to leave, the Corinthians *did not* ask this question:

> Dear Paul, in our community we have some believers who are married to unbelievers. Sometimes the unbelievers have left their Christian spouses. What are they to do now?

If this had been the question that they had asked, Paul would not speak of the believer "allowing" the person to leave because the unsaved person would have already left.

It seems clear, therefore, from Paul's own words (the believer may *allow* the person to leave) that he is not speaking of *desertion by the unbeliever*, but he is speaking of *allowance by the believer*. You see, the Christian is not obligated to fight to keep the unbeliever in the marriage ("God has called us to live in peace," 1 Corinthians 7:15c).

Thus, Paul is not talking about desertion because the issue here is *not about what the unbeliever does*. The issue here is *about what the believer may do*, and that is "allow the unsaved person to leave" (i.e., divorce) if he or she so chooses.

To recap: First, this passage is not addressing married Christians; rather, it is addressing mixed-marriage couples. Second, this passage is not addressing desertion; rather, it is addressing whether or not the believer should allow the unbeliever to leave (i.e., divorce).

What then do we do with Eric and Janna who are both Christians? Paul explains this to us in 1 Corinthians 7:10-11: "To the married I give this command (not I, but the Lord): A wife must not separate from her husband. But *if she does*, she must *remain unmarried* or else *be reconciled to her husband*. And a husband must not divorce his wife" (emphasis mine). Here, then, are the two keys *for married Christians*:

> **Key Number One:** *There is to be no divorce between Christians.*

> **Key Number Two:** If they disobey this command, and they do divorce, then *they must remain unmarried or else be reconciled to each other.*

During our conversation, Pastor John read and reread the verses in question (1 Corinthians 7:10-15). He finally realized that Paul was not talking about desertion at all, and he was not allowing for a Christian couple to divorce and remarry others.

So, he went to Eric and told him that he had given him incorrect advice. He told him that according to Paul, Eric could not date. Eric should remain single and pray for reconciliation with Janna.

About a year later, I saw Pastor John at a restaurant, so I asked how Eric and Janna were doing. He told me that Janna was no longer a member of their church because she was unabashedly living with and having an affair with another man.

So, I asked, "Well then, have you told Eric that he can now date?"

The pastor looked at me dumbfounded and said, "I thought you said that he could not date anyone because Janna and he are both Christians."

I said, "Yes, that's true as long as there is no adultery involved. When Janna left him she had not committed adultery. She didn't leave him for another man. Therefore, the passage that they needed to go by was 1 Corinthians 7:10-11: 'A wife must not separate from her husband. But if she does, she must remain unmarried or else be reconciled to her husband.' However, since Janna has committed adultery against their marriage, Eric's situation now falls under Matthew 19:9 and Matthew 5:32: 'But I tell you that anyone who divorces his wife, except for marital unfaithfulness, causes her to become an adulteress, and anyone who marries the divorced woman commits adultery.' You see, he is now free because of the exception clause: 'except for marital unfaithfulness.' Since Janna has now committed 'marital unfaithfulness,' Eric is no longer bound to her because she is an adulteress. She has sinned against their marriage covenant. Divorcing her will not make her an adulteress because Janna has already become an adulteress by her own sin. And, he will not be committing adultery by remarrying because she is 'dead' to their former marriage covenant due to her adultery."

Do Not Accept One Passage At The Exclusion of Another

As mentioned several times before, one major key of biblical interpretation is that we are not to accept one passage of Scripture to the exclusion of another. When Eric and Janna fit the description that Paul had stated in 1 Corinthians 7, they were bound to his directives therein. However, when Janna sinned against her marriage covenant by committing adultery, they then fell under the description that Jesus gave (Matthew 5:32; 19:9). They were then bound to the words and directives of Jesus which addressed their more recent circumstances.

When in Rome?

In a class I was teaching, a student said that he could not see how it was possible to shift from Paul's instructions to Jesus' instructions just because the circumstances were different. "Isn't this situational ethics?" he asked.

This is a legitimate question, and one that needs to be answered for those who might be confused at this point. In the popular sense, situational (or situation) ethics governs our actions in light of the situation rather than by the application of God's moral absolutes. Christians, however, argue that there are moral absolutes, and we are to live by God's truths and not make our decisions simply based upon the situation that we find ourselves in. In a cliché way, Christians say, "When in Rome, Christians do *not* do as the Romans do. Christians are to do as Christians do in all places, even in Rome."

So, what we must realize is simply this: For the Christian couple who does not commit adultery, the absolute truth of God, *given to us by Paul*, is that they are not to divorce. But, if they do, they are to remain single allowing for a possible reconciliation.

However, for the Christian couple in which one spouse does commit adultery, the absolute truth of God, *given to us by Jesus*, is that the innocent party may divorce the guilty party. So here is the basic difference:

(1) Situation ethics govern human actions in light of the situation, and based upon the philosophy of the highest good for the greatest number of people (at least in theory).

(2) Christian ethics, however, only allows the situation to reveal to us which of God's absolute truths we are to follow.

From Enemies of God to Children of God

Think of it, if this were not true, then no one could call himself or herself a child of God. In one passage of Scripture, the Bible says, "for all have sinned and fall short of the glory of God" (Romans 3:23). Is this an absolute truth? Yes, of course. Romans 3:12 says, "All have turned away, they have together become worthless; there is no one who does good, not even one." The Bible identifies fallen humans as enemies of God (Romans 5:10). Yet, when our circumstances change by accepting Christ as our savior, the Bible says, "Yet to all who received him, to those who believed in his name, he gave the right to become children of God" (John 1:12). Has God's absolute truth that humans are sinners and enemies of God been undone by such a situational change? Not at all. At one time, we were enemies of God, but now we are children of God. So, at one time the verse that applied to me was Romans 3:12. But, then, my circumstances changed in that I accepted Christ as my savior, and the verse that now applies to me is John 1:12.

Likewise, the passage that applied to Eric and Janna was 1 Corinthians 7:10-11: "A wife must not separate from her husband. But if she does, she must remain unmarried or else be reconciled to her husband."

However, instead of being reconciled to her husband, Janna committed adultery. Then the passage that applied to Eric and Janna was Matthew 19:9 "I tell you that anyone who divorces his wife, except for marital unfaithfulness, and marries another woman commits adultery" (as well as Matthew 5:32).

What About Matthew 18?

Knowing the truth of applying various passages that fit various circumstances (as we have shown above), some have taught that if a Christian leaves his or her Christian spouse, then Matthew 18 applies. In Matthew 18:15-18, Jesus says:

> If your brother sins against you, go and show him his fault, just between the two of you. If he listens to you, you have won your brother over. But if he will not listen, take one or two others along, so that 'every matter may be established by the testimony of two or three witnesses.' If he refuses to listen to them, tell it to the church; and if he refuses to listen even to the church, treat him as you would a pagan or a tax collector.

Thus, the application of Matthew 18:15-18 would look like this:

1. Janna divorces Eric.

2. Eric confronts Janna with the sin of divorcing him. If she repents, all is well and good.

3. If, however, she does not repent, then Eric is to take one or two Christians along with him to confront Janna again, so that every matter may be established by the testimony of two or three witnesses.

4. If she repents, all is well and good.

5. If, however, she does not repent, then Eric is to tell the whole church.

6. If she repents, all is well and good.

7. If, however, Janna still refuses to listen even to the church, then they are to treat her as one would treat a pagan or a tax collector.

8. If Janna is now to be treated as a pagan or a tax collector, then Janna and Eric fall under Paul's words in 1 Corinthians chapter 7:15. "But if the unbeliever leaves, let him do so. A believing man or woman is not bound in such circumstances; God has called us to live in peace."

9. Therefore, Eric is now free to remarry because "A believing man or woman is not bound in such circumstances" (1 Corinthians 7:15b).

As seemingly scriptural as this sounds, I do not think that this is correct biblical hermeneutics.[13] Why?

First and foremost, Paul never turned to it. If this were a feasible option, then why didn't Paul simply refer to this portion of Jesus' teachings in 1 Corinthians 7 when he was dealing with the issue of a believer divorcing another believer?

Also, when Jesus says that we are to treat the unrepentant brother who sins against us as we would treat a pagan or a tax collector, it does not mean this brother is no longer a believer. Remember, Jesus says this is how we are to treat a "*brother* who sins against us." This person does not stop being a brother and become an unbeliever, which would

---

[13]Hermeneutics is simply a technical word for "interpretation."

be necessary for 1 Corinthians 7:15 to apply.

Furthermore, I believe that the reason we are to treat an unrepentant brother who sins against us as a pagan or a tax collector is to bring that person ultimately to repentance. Remember, it is reconciliation that is in view in Matthew 18.

So, first, the "brother who sins against us" (Matthew 18) is still a believer. But, the passage in 1 Corinthians 7:15 is talking about an "unbeliever" who leaves. However, when *believers* divorce (without adultery as the cause), the spouses are to remain single or be reconciled to one another (1 Corinthians 7:10-11).

Finally, the entire point of treating an unrepentant brother (or sister) who sins against us as pagan or a tax collector is to bring that person to repentance and reconciliation. Yet, there can be no door left open for reconciliation if the remaining spouse remarries someone else.

So, while it is true that we must be careful to not to accept one passage at the exclusion of another, and that we must know when to shift to which passage when the changing circumstances call for the shift, we must also be careful not to simply grab passages and force them into our situation when they do not truly apply.

Conclusion

Paul allowed no grounds for a Christian to initiate a divorce from a spouse (either a believer or unbeliever) who has been faithful. So, what happens when two Christians do divorce when they're not supposed to? They are to remain single, and neither of them are to date or remarry, unless they date and remarry each other.

However, what happens when one of them does not remain faithful? What if one of them commits adultery or marries someone else? Is the believer then condemned to live his or her life as a single person from that point on? No, at that point, Matthew 19:9 and 5:32 fit his or her particular circumstance.

It is noteworthy that Paul gives different advice for different situations. As a matter of fact Paul gives advice which on the surface might seem different (though not contradictory) from Jesus' teachings. The point is, Jesus did not give the last word on the subject of divorce and remarriage. Knowing that the church would carry on and that there would be issues that would need to be dealt with, Jesus allowed His apostles to cover those issues later under the inspiration of the Holy Spirit as they dealt with real-life situations in their historical context.

In Genesis, God gave the divine order for marriage: one man for one woman. "For this reason a man will leave his father and mother and be united to his wife, and they will become one flesh" (Genesis 2:24).

Then Moses gives a regulation for divorce (*erwat dabar*) in Deuteronomy 24:1-4 (which by the way was given, Jesus said, because of the hardness of men's hearts).

Then in the New Testament, Jesus gives another regulation for divorce, called the exception clause (Matthew 5:32; 19:9).

And Paul gives yet another regulation for divorce in 1 Corinthians 7:15: "But if the unbeliever leaves, let him do so. A believing man or woman is not bound in such circumstances; God has called us to live in peace."

None of these regulations contradict one another. Rather, they build upon each other to give us a mosaic of testimony of the regulations of divorce and remarriage. Because there are multiple regulations, we must be careful not to take only one of them and make it a hard and fast rule for all marital situations.

Study Questions For

Chapter 10
Pastoral Practicalities
Counseling People With Regard to
Divorce and Remarriage

1. Was marriage created by God to make humans happy?

2. In what (or from where) should Christians find their ultimate happiness?

3. If a Christian couple divorces and there is no adultery involved, can they remarry other people?

4. If a Christian couple divorces, and after that, one of the two commits adultery, can the other person remarry someone else?

5. How and when does 1 Corinthians 7:10-11 and Matthew 19:9 and Matthew 5:32 relate to a divorced Christian couple?

6. Why is the principle that we are not to accept one passage at the exclusion of another important with regard to Christian couples who divorce?

7. When we shift from Paul's instructions to Jesus' instructions because the circumstances have changed, is this "situational ethics"? Why or why not?

8. Give the author's reasoning as to why he does not think that it is correct biblical hermeneutics to apply Matthew 18:15-18 to a divorced Christian couple.

9. Did Paul allow grounds for the Christian to initiate a divorce from a spouse who has been faithful?

10. Do the divorce regulations given by Moses, Jesus, and Paul contradict one another? Why or why not?

11. Since there are multiple biblical divorce regulations, what must we be careful not to do?

*Heaven will be no heaven to me if I do not meet
my wife there.—Andrew Jackson*

Chapter 11

The Husband of One Wife

Carl was a bright young man with a calling on his life. He believed that God wanted him to be a pastor. He had been raised in the church, and while at Bible college, he met and fell in love with Sandy. In time, they met each other's families. Their parents were very happy, and soon Carl and Sandy were married.

After they graduated from college, Carl became an associate pastor and began settling into the ministry that he had been pursuing for many years. In only two short years, Carl's ministry activities had helped the small, struggling church double in size. It was still a small church, but things were looking up. However, not all was happy at home.

Sandy became disenchanted with being a pastor's wife. When they had dated in Bible college, Sandy thought that being a pastor's wife would be fun and exciting, and that it would hold some degree of prestige. Instead, she found that it was hard work. She felt like she was under a microscope, and everyone at the church was always evaluating and judging her. She also discovered that her time was not her own. There were always certain women's ministries or Bible studies that she had to attend. Soon, she came to believe that she was not meant to be a pastor's wife after all.

Carl understood Sandy's frustration, and even though he still wanted to be a pastor, for her sake he decided that he would resign from the church and get a "secular job." However, as Sandy thought things over, she decided that it was really more than just being a pastor's wife. She felt like she had married too young, and she wanted the opportunity to date other men. So, without much discussion, and over the objections of her parents, Sandy divorced Carl. Hurt and confused, Carl resigned from the church and took a secular job. He felt that he should not be pastoring others when his own life was falling apart.

Sandy stopped going to church altogether, but Carl found comfort in the church and in the fellowship that he received there. Occasionally, Carl and Sandy would meet for lunch to talk. On one of those occasions, Sandy dropped a bombshell on Carl announcing that she had been dating another man, and they had set the date for their marriage. Soon thereafter, Sandy remarried. Three years later, Carl met a woman at church, and they started dating. About two years after that, they were married.

During this entire time, Carl continued to donate his time and energies to his church. He taught Sunday school and did various things in the church to help the pastoral staff. Now, he felt that God was leading him to return to full-time ministry, but the fellowship of which he was a member held the position that a divorced man who had remarried could not pastor. So, what was he to do? He felt a genuine call of God on his life to be a pastor. After much prayer, Carl and his new wife joined a different church that considered people for ministry on a case-by-case basis. They interviewed Carl and found that he was not the cause of his divorce, so they ordained him, and Carl once again became an associate pastor. More than thirty years have passed since Carl remarried, and he and his wife are still happily married, and they are in ministry together.

Various Interpretations

Paul says to Timothy in 1 Timothy 3:2, and to Titus in Titus 1:6, that an overseer (i.e., pastor, elder, or bishop)[14] must be the husband of one wife. This has been interpreted by various people and churches to mean different things. Let's take a look at Paul's words in context:

1 Timothy 3:1-7

1 It is a trustworthy statement: if any man aspires to the office of overseer [pastor], it is a fine work he desires to do. 2. An overseer, then, must be above reproach, the husband of one wife, temperate, prudent, respectable, hospitable, able to teach, 3 not addicted to wine or pugnacious, but gentle, peaceable, free from the love of money. 4 He must be one who manages his own household well, keeping his children under control with all dignity 5 (but if a man does not know how to manage his own household, how will he take care of the church of God?), 6 and not a new convert, so that he will not become conceited and fall into the condemnation incurred by the devil. 7 And he must have a good reputation with those outside the church, so that he will not fall into reproach and the snare of the devil (NASB).

Titus 1:5-9

5 For this reason I left you in Crete, that you would set in order what remains and appoint elders in every city as I directed you, 6 namely, if any man is above reproach, the husband of one wife, having children who believe, not accused of dissipation or rebellion. 7 For the overseer [pastor or elder] must be above reproach as God's steward, not self-willed, not quick-tempered, not addicted to wine, not pugnacious, not

---

[14] The words *overseer*, *elder*, and *bishop* are virtually synonymous in the Bible and correspond to what we call a *pastor*.

fond of sordid gain, 8 but hospitable, loving what is good, sensible, just, devout, self-controlled, 9 holding fast the faithful word which is in accordance with the teaching, so that he will be able both to exhort in sound doctrine and to refute those who contradict (NASB).

"An overseer [elder or pastor] must be the husband of one wife" says Paul. This one requirement of the pastor is what many people seem to focus on. Interestingly, the fellowship of which Carl was formerly a member allowed people to become pastors when they had not been above reproach, when they had not been self-controlled, when they had not been respectable, when they had not been hospitable, when they had not been able to teach, and when they had not been gentle. In fact, some of their ministers are quarrelsome, and some are lovers of money. Some of them are not able to manage their own families well, and they have rebellious children who disobey them on a consistent basis. However, the one thing that his denomination was absolutely settled on was that no one could be a pastor in their fellowship if he had ever been divorced and remarried.

So, of the many qualifications for a pastor listed by Paul in 1 Timothy 3:1-7 and in Titus 1:5-9, the only one that they seemed to have taken seriously was that "An overseer must be the husband of one wife."

However, we must ask the obvious question. Was Paul referring to the issue of divorce and remarriage in this passage, or was he referring to something else?

The Four Options

Literally in the Greek the words translated as "the husband of one wife" actually say "one woman man." Various Christians understand this phrase to mean different things. There seem to be four basic ideas of what this phrase might mean:

(1) it might be signifying divorce and remarriage
(2) it might be saying single men should not be elders
(3) it might be speaking about marital fidelity
(4) it might be referring to polygamy

This phrase *husband of one wife* is generally interpreted with one's preconceived ideas in mind. If, for instance, a person already believes that a pastor should not be divorced and remarried, then that person will likely interpret this phrase, "husband of one wife," to mean *divorce and remarriage*. Likewise, those who interpret this passage to mean something other than divorce and remarriage are typically not absolutely opposed—in every case—to a person who has been divorced and remarried serving as a pastor. However, I think that the weight of biblical evidence, comparing Scripture with Scripture, can lead us to a solid conclusion without having to get our cue from our preconceived notions.

Idea # 1: Divorce and Remarriage
The position that says Paul was referring to divorce and remarriage in this passage is a rather simple one. Paul said that the pastor must be the husband of one wife. If a man is divorced and remarried, and if his former spouse is still living, then he is by sheer mathematics the husband of two wives. Since Paul said, "one wife," it is obvious (to them) that if a man is divorced and remarried, then he has more than one wife. Their position, then, is that a man can be divorced and continue to be a pastor as long as he does not remarry. If he does not remarry, he stays within the letter of the law and never becomes the husband of more than one wife.

Some have gone even further, arguing that if the man has never been previously married but his wife has, he cannot be an elder. She is—again by sheer mathematics—the wife of two husbands. How exactly they reverse this issue and make the woman's divorce and remarriage an issue of the man's qualifications I am not sure. But, it is intriguing nonetheless to see how far some people will go in placing legalistic rules upon themselves (and others) that God never established.

How Jesus' Teachings Relate

As most people know, in the Old Testament when a woman committed adultery, she was stoned to death. This, then, obviously, allowed for the man to remarry. Thus, he was still the husband of only one wife because his first wife was dead.

However, in the New Testament (because of Roman law) there was a shift away from putting the adulterer to death. And, in our day and culture people are not put to death for adultery. Yet, it does seem biblically consistent to think of the adulterer as "being dead" as far as the marriage covenant is concerned, and this is why Jesus said that one may divorce an adulterous spouse. Furthermore, the innocent party may also remarry (Matthew 5:32; 19:9).

Now, if the innocent party who was divorced from his adulterous wife was really still married to her, why would Jesus allow that person to get remarried? Would Jesus have promoted multiple wives? Obviously not. For all intents and purposes, the adulterer has broken the marriage covenant and is "dead" to his or her spouse. When the innocent party remarries, he or she is at that point married to only one spouse, not two, because the first spouse has "died" (metaphorically speaking). Paul talks about people being able to remarry after their spouses have died physically:

> Do you not know, brothers—for I am speaking to men who know the law—that the law has authority over a man only as long as he lives? For example, by law a married woman is bound to her husband as long as he is alive, but if her husband dies, she is released from the law of marriage. So then, if she marries another man while her husband is still alive, she is called an adulteress. But if her husband dies, she is released from that law and is not an adulteress, even though she marries another man (Romans 7:1-3).

So, even if Paul's statement "an overseer must be the husband of one wife" is referring to the concept of divorce and remarriage (which is debatable, as we shall see later), it seems obvious that it would have to be an illegitimate (i.e., unscriptural) divorce and remarriage that would keep the man from being a pastor. Note well that it was Jesus Himself who gave the famous *exception clause* (Matthew 5:32, 19:9). However, if a man divorces a wife who has not committed adultery, the wife is not "dead" to the marriage covenant. Thus, Jesus says that the one who divorces his wife *causes her to become an adulteress.* Furthermore, he says that anyone who marries the divorced woman also commits adultery.

Certainly it would be appropriate to exclude a man from ministry who has divorced his wife and remarried without scriptural warrant. When there is no scriptural warrant for the divorce, the spouses are to remain single or be reconciled to one another (1 Corinthians 7:10-11).

However, if a woman divorces her husband without scriptural warrant and then marries another man (as in the case of Carl and Sandy mentioned above), then she has committed adultery, and the man is then free to remarry since she is now "dead" to their former marriage covenant, and he is no longer married to his first spouse. And even though he enters into a second marriage, the man is the husband of only one wife because his first wife is "dead" to him and to their prior marriage covenant.

Is It Divorce and Remarriage?

Paul says: "the overseer must be . . . the husband of one wife" (1 Timothy 3:1-2). It is interesting, and likely instructive, that Paul does not use the words "divorced and remarried." He does not say, "Now the overseer must never have been divorced and remarried." He says that "the overseer must be the husband of one wife."

The idea that this phrase "the husband of one wife" means "divorced and remarried" is simply an *interpretation* of the phrase, not a translation of it. There is nothing in the context or in the very words themselves to positively conclude that this means the overseer (pastor) must not have been divorced and remarried. And, as stated above, even if Paul had literally said "divorced and remarried," it would seem biblical—given the various other regulations about divorce and remarriage—that it would have to be limited to a scripturally unjustified divorce and remarriage. Else, why would Jesus even allow for divorce *and remarriage* (Matthew 5:32; 19:9), and why would Paul say that if the unbeliever is set on leaving, let him/her go, and that the innocent spouse in this situation is not under bondage (1 Corinthians 7:15)? It seems logically inconsistent for Jesus to allow for divorce and remarriage when the spouse has committed adultery, but yet at the same time hold that divorce and remarriage against the innocent spouse later.

Divorce and Remarriage Before Conversion

Another teaching that needs to be addressed is the faulty idea that if a man was divorced and remarried prior to his conversion to Christ, then he is not held to 1 Timothy 3:2. This, of course, falls under the teachings of those who see 1 Timothy 3:2 as speaking of divorce and remarriage. This is a most illogical and non-scriptural position. Those who argue for this say that if a Christian man has been divorced and remarried, he is disqualified from being an elder (pastor) due to 1 Timothy 3:2. However, if a non-Christian man has been divorced and remarried, and then he comes to salvation in Christ, he is not disqualified from be an elder (pastor) due to 1 Timothy 3:2. In other words, the grace of God extends further for sinners than for His own children. Somehow those who hold this view wish to promote the idea that it is an issue of knowledge. The Christian man "should have known better," while the non-Christian man is not accountable for his lack of knowledge about the sins of divorce and remarriage.

However, addressing the worship of false gods, Scripture says, "In the past God overlooked such ignorance, but now he commands all people everywhere to repent" (Acts 17:30). The point seems to be that man is not "given a pass" for his sins because of his ignorance. Besides this, can we be sure that every man who was divorced and remarried prior to his conversion really did not know that a selfish divorce and remarriage was wrong? Hardly.

Next, Paul certainly does not agree that God forgives only sinners. God forgives Christians who sin as well. Paul says,

> But God demonstrates his own love for us in this: While we were still sinners, Christ died for us. Since we have now been justified by his blood, how much more shall we be saved from God's wrath through him! For if, when we were God's enemies, we were reconciled to him through the death of his Son, how much more, having been reconciled, shall we be saved through his life! (Romans 5:8-10).

Note well that if when we were God's enemies, we were reconciled to him through the death of Jesus, *how much more* now that we are His children shall we be saved through his life! Then the apostle John writes:

> If we claim we have not sinned, we make him out to be a liar and his word has no place in our lives. My dear children, I write this to you so that you will not sin. But if anybody does sin, *we have one who speaks to the Father in our defense*—Jesus Christ, the Righteous One. He is the atoning sacrifice for our sins, and not only for ours but also for the sins of the whole world (emphasis mine, 1 John 1:10—2:2).

"We have one who speaks to the Father in our defense" (1 John 2:1b). It is simply a man-contrived idea, with no scriptural warrant, that says that there is a clean slate for the non-Christian man who has been divorced and remarried, but there is no clean slate for the Christian man who has been divorced and remarried. There is not a single verse that says if a man is a non-Christian and he is divorced and remarried he can still be an elder but that if a man is already a Christian and then he gets divorced and remarried, he cannot be an elder. This "divorced and remarried before conversion" idea is faulty at its core (i.e., forgiveness only for sinners), and it hasn't one verse of Scripture to commend it.

Idea # 2 Single Men Should not be Elders

This position is less popular than the preceding one. Nonetheless, some people see in Paul's words, "the husband of one wife" the idea of simply being married. If a man is single, then he is not the husband of one wife. In fact, he is not a husband at all, and, according to this position, he does not fulfill the *requirement* of having one wife. This position is buttressed by the fact that Paul goes on to say, "He must be one who manages his own household well, keeping his children under control with all dignity (but if a man does not know how to manage his own household, how will he take care of the church of God?)" (1 Timothy 3:4-5). How can the man demonstrate that he can keep his children under control and manage his family if he is not even married? Those who hold this position see marriage as a necessity that allows one to demonstrate that he is a mature person who can, ultimately, manage the church of God.

While a man can gain valuable experience through marriage, and while raising children is a proving ground for growth in maturity, there seems to be no corroborating biblical warrant to believe that the phrase "The husband of one wife" means that one *must be* married.

Certainly Paul would have the elders be mature believers; he says as much when he goes on to say that the elder should not be "a new convert, so that he will not become conceited and fall into the condemnation incurred by the devil" (1 Timothy 3:6). But, it appears that the idea that a man *must be married* to be an elder is simply an interpretation of this passage that is not supported by the immediate context or by corroborating passages of Scripture.

Idea # 3 Marital Fidelity

A third interpretation that some have proposed takes

the phrase much more literally (from the Greek) and suggests that 1 Timothy 3:2 is simply saying that an elder must be a "one-woman man." That is to say that the pastor must not be a womanizer or a flirt. He must be a man who has control of his passions and is faithful to his wife. He must be a man who is devoted to his wife, not a philanderer or a "skirt chaser."

I believe that this interpretation is far more feasible than the first two. After all, the Bible talks frequently about fidelity in marriage and keeping one's passions under control. While this interpretation may or may not necessarily be correct precisely for 1 Timothy 3:2, it is nonetheless correct overall as a requirement for any Christian and especially for the leaders within the church.

Idea # 4 Polygamy

Often those who hold the position that the phrase "the husband of one wife" means divorce and remarriage also argue that polygamy was not an issue at the time of Paul's writing. Therefore, Paul had no need or reason to address it. However, even a little research on the history of polygamy among the Jews shows that polygamy was in fact an accepted practice and a problem in Paul's day among the Jews and for many centuries after the time of Paul.

Perhaps the confusion about this comes from the fact that polygamy was not typically practiced in the Roman world outside Palestine. In fact, what seems to be contra-logical, the Romans were against polygamy while the Jews favored and practiced it. Reading the various writers on this issue, many over generalize the issue and say something like this:

> Since polygamy was against Roman law, and the Jews were under Roman law, there would be no need for Paul to have addressed polygamy in 1 Timothy 3:1-2. Therefore, he must have been talking about divorce and remarriage.

However, this is an oversimplification of the culture of the Jews in general and of polygamy in particular in New

Testament times. Yes, Roman law was against polygamy, but the Jews were not, and they did not simply adapt to all Roman laws.

> There is evidence of the practice of polygamy in Palestinian Judaism in NT times . . . . Herod the Great (37-4 B.C.) had ten wives . . . and a considerable harem . . . Polygamy and concubinage among the aristocracy is attested by Josephus [A.D. 37-100] . . . The continued practice of levirate marriage . . . evidently led to polygamy, which was countenanced [condoned] by the school of Shammai but not by that of Hillel. . . . According to the investigations of H. Grandqvist, in the village of Aretas near Bethlehem twelve out of 112 married men had more than one wife . . . .[15]

And, this is not the only set of testimonies to the issue of polygamy in Jewish culture during the New Testament times, nor of the ongoing issues that Christian leaders had to deal with in regard to polygamy. But even from these alone, it is obvious that polygamy was indeed an issue before, during, and after Paul's day.

The quote above says that "in the village of Aretas near Bethlehem twelve out of 112 married men had more than one wife." Thus, in this one village alone nearly 11% of the marriages were polygamous! Those who say that polygamy was not an issue in New Testament times are simply ignoring the historical evidence. Polygamy was most certainly an issue in New Testament times and beyond.

So, is it any wonder that Paul had to write that "An overseer, then, must be above reproach, the husband of one wife"? (1 Timothy 3:2). As Jews continued to put their faith in Jesus as Messiah, Paul had to make clear that those Jewish

---

[15] *The New International Dictionary of New Testament Theology*, Colin Brown, ed., s.v. "Marriage, Adultery, Bride, Bridegroom," Vol 2. (Grand Rapids, MI: Zondervan, 1986), pp. 578-579.

Christians in polygamous marriages could not be elders (pastors) in the church. Only those who were the "husband of one wife" could serve in that capacity.

Having an implied pro-monogamous stance from Jesus on this issue, Paul would be bound to make sure that the church knew and recognized God's original intent for marriage. Jesus said, "For this reason *a man* will leave his father and mother and be united to his *wife*, and the *two* will become *one* flesh. So they are no longer two, but one. Therefore what God has joined together, let man not separate" (emphasis mine, Matthew 19: 5-6). Since one of the primary rules governing marriage was that it must be one man and one woman, God would not want people in positions of authority who had multiple wives. Marriage should be monogamous.

Interestingly, while polygamy (plural marriage) is a recognized fact of the Old Testament, the law forbade polygamy for the *kings* of Israel (Deuteronomy 17:17). However, it was not forbidden for the average Israelite. So, just as God set standards for the leadership of Israel that He did not require of the average Israelite, so too in the New Testament God sets standards for the leadership of the church that He does not require of the average Christian. Since polygamy was still practiced by many early Jewish Christians, Paul had to reiterate God's standard for leadership, i.e., monogamy. Note the issue of multiple wives in Deuteronomy 17:17 in comparison with 1 Timothy 3:2:

> **The king,** moreover, must not acquire great numbers of horses for himself or make the people return to Egypt to get more of them, for the LORD has told you, "You are not to go back that way again." He **must not take many wives**, or his heart will be led astray. He must not accumulate large amounts of silver and gold (emphasis mine, Deuteronomy 17:16-17).

> **An overseer,** then, **must be** above reproach, **the husband of one wife,** temperate, prudent, respectable, hospitable, able to teach" (emphasis mine, 1 Timothy

3:2, NASB).

Note the key words in these two passages:

The king must not take many wives

An overseer must be the husband of one wife.

Thus, those who hold the position that the phrase "the husband of one wife" refers to polygamy argue that when men who were in polygamous marriages came to the Lord, they were not required to divest themselves of all but one wife, but neither were they allowed to be in a position of leadership in the church. Only a man who was "the husband of one wife," i.e., monogamous, could serve as an elder (pastor).

This interpretation makes perfect sense, especially in light of the fact that there is Old Testament precedent requiring the leaders of Israel to be monogamous (although not all of them obeyed this regulation), and in light of the fact that polygamy was a serious issue in Paul's day.

The position that the phrase "the husband of one wife" refers to polygamy is also more consistent with the balance of Scripture, e.g., Jesus' teaching concerning the exception clause, Paul's statement about a believing spouse being free from the unbelieving spouse who leaves.

While every elder certainly must demonstrate marital fidelity, I do not think that this is what Paul was specifically addressing in 1 Timothy 3:2.

I believe that given the fact that polygamy was a real issue during the New Testament, and given the fact that the Old Testament had already set the precedent of leaders not having multiple marriages, that 1 Timothy 3:2 is referring to polygamy rather than to divorce and remarriage, which Moses, Jesus, and Paul all allowed under certain circumstances.

Going Beyond The Holiness of God

I know that "Going Beyond The Holiness of God" seems like an impossibility. After all, God is the most holy.

But, what I mean by "Going Beyond The Holiness of God" is that people often set standards "higher" than what God has set. Perhaps a better word than "higher" would be "more stringent." People in cults do this all the time by setting good works as a requirement for salvation. Yet, every true believer knows that it is not by his or her good works that he or she is saved, but it is by the good work of the Savior Jesus Christ.

Another word for "Going Beyond The Holiness of God" is *legalism.* Too often Christians add all sorts of rules and regulations that God never set nor intended. In one church I attended many years ago, I was told that I had to shave my mustache because it was a sin to have facial hair. A friend once told me that when she became a member of a certain church, she had to sign a statement of "Do's and Don'ts" and the "Don'ts" outnumbered the "Do's" four to one. I do not recall all of the "Don'ts" she listed, but one was "don't attend a movie at a public movie theater." However, when the movie "Jesus" came out later that year, even her pastor attended the movie *at a public movie theater*!

Well-meaning men sometimes add extra rules and regulations (i.e., legalism) to the Bible's teachings. For example, I believe that the teaching that "the husband of one wife" unqualifiedly means divorce and remarriage is nothing more than man's imposed legalism.

When we set our own requirements and restrictions for Christians and Christian ministers beyond what God has established for them, we have moved from His righteousness to *self-righteousness*. This was the sin of the Pharisees. When we set our own standards of holiness, and when we attempt to impose our standards on others, we will always develop artificial boundaries, and we will take great pride in observing them. What was meant to keep us holy, i.e., these extra rules and regulations, becomes a point of pride when we live up to them. And, then, the sins of legalism and pride generally lead to unmitigated arrogance.

Our goal should be to find out what God actually said and live by His rules and not by man-made rules and regulations.

Study Questions For

Chapter 11
The Husband of One Wife

1. Briefly list the four interpretations of Paul's words, "the husband of one wife."
2. Give the verse of Scripture that says that if a man is a non-Christian and he is divorced and remarried and then becomes a Christian, he can still be an elder. But, if a man is already a Christian and then he gets divorced and remarried, he cannot be an elder.
3. Do you believe that "the husband of one wife" refers to divorce and remarriage? Why or why not?
4. Do you believe that "the husband of one wife" refers to the idea that single men should not be elders? Why or why not?
5. Do you believe that "the husband of one wife" refers to the idea of marital fidelity, i.e., a "one-woman man"? Why or Why not?
6. Do you believe that "the husband of one wife" refers to monogamy as opposed to polygamy? Why or Why not?
7. What does the author mean by "Going Beyond The Holiness of God"?
8. When we set our own requirements and restrictions beyond what God has established, what have we moved from, and what have we moved to?
9. How do our own standards of holiness lead us into unmitigated arrogance?
10. Concerning God's rules, what should our goal be?

He who does not honour his wife,
dishonours himself.—Spanish Proverb

Chapter 12

Spousal Abuse

Can a Man Break Faith by Abuse?

The man had kept his wife shackled in their basement for 12 years. Somehow he had managed to alienate her entire family so they were never allowed to see her. Therefore, they had no idea what had been going on.

On occasion, the man beat his wife so violently that he broke some of her bones. Because he would not allow her to receive medical treatment, her bones fused together improperly.

He used and abused her as a sex slave, subjecting her to the most depraved sexual deviations imaginable.

He would leave her alone for days without the proper use of bathroom facilities. Like a chained animal she had to endure the putrefaction of her own excrement. Insects crawled on her day and night.

She rarely saw the light of day. When she was allowed out of the basement, her husband kept her on a leash.

Due to the extreme and continued abuse, she fell into manic depression and thoughts of suicide constantly filled her mind.

Finally, somehow, the police became aware of the woman's plight and soon thereafter brought this horrendous situation to a halt.

I am not sure how anyone can say that this woman did not have biblical grounds for divorce. I believe that this man broke the loving marriage covenant that he had entered into at the time of their wedding. Had he committed adultery? No. But, what he did do was no less a breaking of the bond of marriage.

I believe that spousal abuse is grounds for divorce when the abuse is so destructive that the "one flesh" bond between husband and wife has been broken. (I will discuss the "one flesh" bond more below.) Though historically and contextually Malachi was talking about an unlawful divorce, I think the *principle* behind his words can apply to the abusive situation as well. The prophet says,

> . . . the LORD is acting as the witness between you and the wife of your youth, because you have broken faith with her, though she is your partner, the wife of your marriage covenant. Has not the LORD made them one? In flesh and spirit they are his. And why one? Because he was seeking godly offspring. So guard yourself in your spirit, and do not break faith with the wife of your youth (Malachi 2:14-15).

Is adultery the only way for a man to "break faith with his wife"? I do not believe so. In Malachi 2:16 God says, "I hate divorce." But, wouldn't God also say, "I hate spousal abuse"? I think so, especially in light of the Scripture's declaration: "Husbands, love your wives, just as Christ loved the church and gave himself up for her" (5:25).

Spousal Abuse Defined

Spousal abuse is defined simply as the deliberate attempt by a spouse to control or intimidate his or her partner. While most abusers are men, there are women who are also abusive. No one knows exactly how wide spread or serious husband-abuse is. Part of the reason may lie with the fact that most men are too embarrassed to admit that they are being abused by their wives. However, while husband-abuse does exist, the vast majority of cases of spousal abuse is committed against women; therefore, this chapter will follow that emphasis.

Spousal abuse is not limited to just the physical. It certainly includes physical abuse, but it may include psychological, sexual, and even financial abuse (as it relates to the psychological subjugation of the wife). Often when a woman is abused, it is rarely limited to just one form. Let's look briefly at some forms of abuse.

Physical Abuse

Physical abuse is also known as assault and can include a variety of things such as beatings, burning, cutting, kicking, pinching, placing in captivity, pulling hair, punching, pushing, shooting, slapping, stabbing, and more.

Psychological

Psychological abuse is more difficult to quantify than physical abuse. While you can see and take pictures of the bruises, cuts, or burns left from physical abuse, psychological abuse leaves no such physical tracks. It is no less real or destructive however. Psychological abuse can include threats, unrelenting criticism, obsessive control of activities and friends, humiliation, screaming, threat of physical abuse, obsessive control of money whereby the spouse controls the partner, and more.

Financial

Financial abuse is more than simply the husband taking control of the finances of the home. It can include controlling the finances to such a degree that the wife cannot get necessary food or medical treatment without his explicit permission. Financial abuse may be a subset under psychological abuse. However, should the withholding of money cause the wife not to get the proper food or medical treatment that she needs, it can also fall under physical abuse.

Sexual

Sexual abuse is sexual touching or intercourse that is not consensual. Some men have the idea that if they are married, they can simply gratify themselves sexually even when their spouses say no. This, in short, is rape, and it is not normal marital sexual relations. A husband must never force himself upon his wife.

Grounds for Divorce?

While it is easy to list (as I have done above) some of the forms of spousal abuse, a subsequent issue is far more difficult to discover and explain. That is, do some forms of abuse rise to the level of biblical grounds for divorce? Simply put, does a wife have scriptural grounds to divorce her husband if he is abusive to her?

There are those who argue that only adultery is grounds for divorce. They point out that nowhere does Jesus or Paul say that a woman can divorce her husband due to spousal abuse. This argument says if the Bible does not address it, then you cannot do it.

It is true enough that there is no direct word from the Lord or from one of the New Testament writers that says plainly, "Spousal abuse is grounds for divorce." However, it is just as true that there is no direct word from the Lord or from one of the New Testament writers that says plainly, "Spousal abuse is *not* grounds for divorce."[16]

So, are we left in a seemingly precarious situation? It seems apparent that what we must do is look at the entirety of Scripture and ask ourselves, "What is the tenor (i.e., the general sense) of Scripture on this topic?" In other words, what is the *spirit of the law*, not just the *letter of the law,* concerning the issue of marriage, spousal abuse, and divorce?

The Occasion of Paul's Writing to the Corinthians

Note well that Paul's address to the Corinthians was in response to various issues that were raised by reports that he

---

[16] It might be instructive to point out that there is also no direct word from the Lord or from one of the Old Testament or New Testament writers that says plainly, "God is a Trinity." Yet, the doctrine of the Christian Trinity is an exegetically and theologically established fundamental doctrine of Christian orthodoxy.

had received from people in the Corinthian church. In other words, Paul had heard some things that disturbed him, and he had also received a letter from the Christians at Corinth in which they asked him specific questions about divorce and remarriage.

When one views the entire letter to the Corinthians, it appears that Paul had multiple reasons for writing to them. One was to deal with the moral issues and divisions in the Corinthian church (1:10). Another purpose was to defend his own apostolic authority (4:1-21). And, another was that he was responding directly to specific questions that the Corinthians had asked him in a letter (7:1), and there were other issues as well.

So, what might be the reason Paul never addressed the issue of spousal abuse? It may be as simple as the fact that the Corinthians never asked him about it. One wonders what Paul might have said if the Corinthians had asked him the question, *"Does a woman have the right to divorce an abusive husband?"*

In a recent televised debate, a man stated that Jesus was not against homosexuality because He never addressed it. In his thinking, as long as the Lord Jesus had not spoken against it, then it was acceptable sexual behavior. His opponent then pointed out that Jesus also never addressed the issue of incest. You see, just because Jesus never addressed it does not make it OK. What is the tenor (i.e., the general sense) of the Bible on the subject of incest? What is the tenor of the Bible on the subject of homosexuality? And, what is the tenor of the Bible on the subject of spousal abuse?

As an analytical thinker, I like things that are either black or white, and right or wrong. I like that *two plus two always equal four*, and if someone says otherwise, I know that he is mistaken. I like it when the Bible is openly clear on an issue. Jesus said, "I tell you that anyone who divorces his wife, except for marital unfaithfulness, and marries another woman commits adultery" (Matthew 19:9). I like that passage because it is clear. However, when we talk of spousal abuse and if it is grounds for divorce and remarriage, we must shift from obvious analysis to scriptural implications and thoughtful, educated inferences.

The One Flesh Bond between Husband and Wife

At the beginning of this chapter, I recounted a scenario of spousal abuse. I think that most would agree the abused wife described therein would have grounds for divorce. I believe that spousal abuse can be grounds for divorce when the abuse is so destructive that the "one-flesh" bond between husband and wife has been broken.

> "Haven't you read," he replied, "that at the beginning the Creator 'made them male and female,' and said, 'For this reason a man will leave his father and mother and be united to his wife, and the two will become one flesh'? So they are no longer two, but one. Therefore what God has joined together, let man not separate" (Matthew 19:4-6).

Jesus taught us that a man and a woman become one flesh. What, then, are the implications of this oneness? Paul addresses this in Ephesians.

> Wives, submit to your husbands as to the Lord. For the husband is the head of the wife as Christ is the head of the church, his body, of which he is the Savior. Now as the church submits to Christ, so also wives should submit to their husbands in everything. Husbands, love your wives, just as Christ loved the church and gave himself up for her to make her holy, cleansing her by the washing with water through the word, and to present her to himself as a radiant church, without stain or wrinkle or any other blemish, but holy and blameless. In this same way, husbands ought to love their wives as their own bodies. He who loves his wife loves himself. After all, no one ever hated his own body, but he feeds and cares for it, just as Christ does the church—for we are members of his body. "For

this reason a man will leave his father and mother and be united to his wife, and the two will become one flesh." This is a profound mystery—but I am talking about Christ and the church. However, each one of you also must love his wife as he loves himself, and the wife must respect her husband (Ephesians 5:22-33).

Love Your Wives

This passage, Ephesians 5:22-33, tells us what it means to be "one flesh." There are several key elements here that we must review. First, Paul says:

Husbands, love your wives, just as Christ loved the church and gave himself up for her to make her holy, cleansing her by the washing with water through the word, and to present her to himself as a radiant church, without stain or wrinkle or any other blemish, but holy and blameless (5:25-27).

When a man abuses his wife, he is certainly not loving her as Christ loved the church.

In fact, Paul says that Christ "gave himself up for her." In other words, Jesus placed the church's needs before His own. How did Christ give Himself up for the church? He died for her. Far from abusing the church, Jesus allowed Himself to be abused in her place. Isaiah tells us what this was like:

Surely he took up our infirmities and carried our sorrows, yet we considered him stricken by God, smitten by him, and afflicted. But he was pierced for our transgressions, he was crushed for our iniquities; the punishment that brought us peace was upon him, and by his wounds we are healed. We all, like sheep, have gone astray, each of us has turned to his own way; and the LORD has laid on him the iniquity of us all (Isaiah 53:4-6).

Husbands are to love their wives as Christ loved the church, *and Christ died for the church*. Not only did Christ die for the church, but He suffered the wrath of God almighty on her behalf. This is not given to us as an option. It is the command of Scripture. Can a man truly be said to be loving his wife as Christ loved the church if he is abusing her? Obviously not.

Furthermore, love is demonstrated. God did not just tell humanity that He loved us. He demonstrated it to us. "But God demonstrates his own love for us in this: While we were still sinners, Christ died for us" (Romans 5:8). And, the Gospel of John tells us,

> For God so loved the world that he gave his one and only Son, that whoever believes in him shall not perish but have eternal life. For God did not send his Son into the world to condemn the world, but to save the world through him (John 3:16-17).

He *demonstrated* His love to us by giving and sending His unique Son to die for us. Think of how it would have been had Christ abused the church the way that many husbands abuse their wives. Would the church respond in love and worship? Certainly not.

Husbands Are To Be A Shelter From The Storm

In the old Testament, there were false religions whose gods were fierce, angry, and vengeful. The adherents of these false religions were cowering slaves who saw their gods as divine tyrants from whom to hide. Christianity, however, sees God as *the shelter from the storm*. David talks of this in the Psalms:

> He who dwells in the shelter of the Most High will rest in the shadow of the Almighty. I will say of the LORD, "He is my refuge and my fortress, my God, in whom I trust." Surely he will save you from the fowler's snare and from the deadly pestilence. He will cover you with his feathers, and under his wings you will find refuge;

his faithfulness will be your shield and rampart. You will not fear the terror of night, nor the arrow that flies by day, nor the pestilence that stalks in the darkness, nor the plague that destroys at midday (Psalm 91:1-6).

For a husband to love his wife as Christ loved the church, he must be her shelter, her refuge, and her fortress. He must be the shelter to which she can run to be protected from the storms of life. However, when a husband abuses his wife, he *is* the storm. And, when the husband is the storm, to where can she run for protection?

It is a powerful testimony that the same context in which Paul commands men to love their wives as Christ loved the church he also talks about the reality of the "one flesh" that is husband and wife:

> In this same way, husbands ought to love their wives as their own bodies. He who loves his wife loves himself. After all, no one ever hated his own body, but he feeds and cares for it, just as Christ does the church (Ephesians 5:28-29).

When a man abuses his wife, he is openly demonstrating that he does not truly love her. Years ago, I heard a preacher say,

> It is fascinating that Paul first says that men are to love their wives as Christ loved the church. But then almost as if he intuitively knows that some men cannot live up to such a high standard, he drops that analogy and moves to a lesser one. Paul goes on to say, "And if you cannot love your wife as Christ loved the church, you should at least love her as much as you do your own body."

I believe that the preacher missed Paul's intent entirely. Certainly a man who loves his wife as much as he does his own body would not abuse her. However, what Paul does with the original analogy is to develop it to the next logical step.

Note the last part of verse 29, *"but he feeds and cares for it, just as Christ does the church."* Paul has not left his original analogy here, nor has he given a lesser analogy of body-love. What Paul has done is taken it to the next step. First Christ died for the church and bought her with His very death on the cross. Then, after that, *He feeds and cares for the church.* This is an ongoing process of love. In reality, what Paul seems to be doing is saying that after the honeymoon is over and you move into real life, that's when you continue to love your wife and you take care of her as you would your own body, just as Christ does with His body. Jesus demonstrated His love for His church by dying for her, and He *continues* to demonstrate His love for her by *continuing* to take care of her as He feeds her and cares for her; and husbands, *you are to do the same.*

Love, then, is not a one-time act. It is an ongoing decision to demonstrate continued care and love. Certainly the abusive husband is not living up to this kind of love. He is not loving his wife as Christ loved the church.

A Tall Order To Fill

Now, all husbands, if they are honest (and all wives for that matter) will admit that they do not love their spouses as much as they should. We husbands are not perfect as Christ is. To love as Christ loved is a tall order to fill. No husband is perfect in his love for his wife as Christ is in His love for the church. But, not living up to the highest possible standard is a far cry from actual abuse. Husbands who truly love their wives deeply regret that they are not better husbands and that they do not love their wives with a more pure love. Men who abuse their wives do not care to be better husbands, and they do not want to love their wives more. Men who abuse their wives turn Paul's words in 1 Corinthians 13:4-8 upside down. Abusive husbands are not patient. They are not kind. They envy and boast. They are prideful. They are rude and self-seeking, and they are easily angered. They keep record of wrongs. They delight in the evil of abuse and hide from the truth. They do not protect their wives; they never trust them; their affection does not persevere, and their love fails.

Next Paul quotes the Lord when he says, "For this reason a man will leave his father and mother and be united to his wife, and the two will become one flesh" (Ephesians 5:31). One flesh. This is the key. A man is to be *one flesh* with his spouse. Would a normal man abuse his own body? No. Therefore, he is not to abuse his wife who is now one flesh with him and he with her. This one flesh is a unity that is only achieved through the covenant of marriage, and if the abuser breaks this one-flesh bond through spousal abuse, he may in fact be breaking his marriage covenant.

So, while it is true that there is no passage that simply and clearly says that "spousal abuse is grounds for divorce," there seems to be an obvious sense within Scripture that spousal abuse may indeed be grounds for divorce. It is my personal conclusion that spousal abuse can be grounds for divorce if the abuse is serious enough to break the one-flesh bond, which was entered into by the marriage covenant.

Furthermore, if you would agree with me that the woman who was chained in her basement and severely beaten and sexually abused for 12 years had grounds for divorce, then the question is not, "Is spousal abuse grounds for divorce?" The question really is, "How bad does the abuse have to be before a woman has grounds for divorce?"

Where Are The Limits

It is impossible for a person to pen exactly what abuse rises to a level that is grounds for divorce. And, certainly we must never use spousal abuse as a catch-all excuse for divorce. I know some pastors are afraid to tell their congregations that they believe spousal abuse is grounds for divorce because they fear that too many people will attempt to use it simply as an excuse for divorce when it is not truly warranted.

After all, what husband has not been a jerk from time to time? We may, I think, reverse that as well. What wife is perfect and has never resorted to psychological warfare during a marital fight? The mere fact that we are humans and that we are fallen creatures—even though we may be born-again—dictates that we will be abusive to one another in one way or another on occasion. The goal, of course, is sanctification in our marriages as well as in our daily walk with the Lord. In brief, the goal of the husband is to love his wife as Christ loved the church.

Do husbands always demonstrate that pure love? Of course not. I have seen well-mannered men who deeply love and respect their wives have a very bad day. Something triggers a flood of negative emotions, and the wife ends up being the brunt of his anger. I have also witnessed well-mannered women who deeply love and respect their husbands, who under similar stressful situations have done the same sort of thing to their husbands.

Is this behavior fair to either spouse? Certainly not. Am I excusing this sort of behavior? Absolutely not. However, is this occasional, negative psychological or emotional lashing out grounds for divorce? No.

So, how do we set the limits? Occasional yelling and physical intimidation certainly do not seem to be grounds for divorce. But what if he takes it to the next level and actually hits his wife? Is that grounds for divorce? What if he only does it one time?

And, what about the wife who occasionally gives her husband the silent treatment when she's angry, or withholds normal marital relations as a form of punishment? Those too are certainly forms of spousal abuse, but do they rise to grounds for divorce? Or, does she have to do it seven times, or seventy times seven?

As you can see, this chapter will not be able to indicate where the parameters are. This chapter can only make broad suggestions and broad conclusions. It is my personal belief that spousal abuse can be grounds for divorce. However, it is also my belief that it would take marital counseling with a professional and well-qualified Christian counselor to help a couple walk through the full range of issues to determine if what a spouse is subjected to is in fact grounds for divorce.

Child Abuse

Another aspect of abuse is child abuse. Shall a woman

stay in a marriage in which the husband physically or sexually abuses his children? I would say no. And, while others may agree with that, they might also argue that though the wife should remove her children and herself from such a destructive situation, she still does not have grounds for remarriage. Yet, it is altogether likely that if a wife justifiably removes her children and herself from an abusive husband, it will not be long before that husband starts dating other women. Once he does, he commits adultery. Then the woman would have grounds for divorce and remarriage, due to Jesus' exception clause, Matthew 5:32; 19:9.

Again, let me reiterate that I am *not* advocating divorce simply because your spouse is a jerk or an insensitive slob, which you might deem as abusive. Abuse that would rise to the level of grounds for divorce must break the one-flesh bond between husband and wife, and this can only be determined by taking a goodly amount of time, praying about it, and discussing it with a qualified counselor. Also, I would suggest that the husband be part of the counseling because it might be something that he can change once he is called into account.

Desertion as Grounds for Divorce

A curious reason often given for divorce and remarriage is desertion. I say that this is curious because it is often the case that those who talk of desertion as grounds for divorce are the same ones who deny spousal abuse as grounds for divorce.

Simply stated, the idea of desertion is when a man moves out of the family home and no longer stays in contact with the wife. What makes this more curious is that those who argue for desertion as grounds for divorce often cite Paul's words where he says, "But if the unbeliever leaves, let him do so. A believing man or woman is not bound in such circumstances; God has called us to live in peace" (1 Corinthians 7:15). However, this passage seems to be saying more about "allowance" than "desertion." Paul does not say that once a Christian is "deserted," he or she is free. What he says is if the unbeliever wants to leave, the Christian should allow that person to leave, and then he or she is free.

Now, I too would see true desertion as grounds for divorce and remarriage, but I won't turn to 1 Corinthians 7:15 and twist Paul's words to arrive at that conclusion. It seems better to see the concept of marriage in the overall tenor of Scripture and make the determination about desertion on that basis rather than manipulating a text for that purpose. Certainly one who deserts his spouse is not loving her as Christ loved the church, and by his desertion he has broken the marriage covenant.

Next, some people have taken Paul's words in 1 Corinthians 7:15 to even further extremes. Some argue that when a husband abuses his wife so badly that it is impossible to live with him any longer, it is called "constructive desertion." What is "constructive desertion"? That's when the abusive situation is the "equivalent of desertion." So, amazingly, from Paul's words about allowing the unbeliever to leave, some have concluded that desertion and extreme spousal abuse are grounds for divorce; but, they don't call it spousal abuse, they euphemize it and call it "constructive desertion." I think we should call it what it really is, *spousal abuse*. We need not do eisegetical gymnastics to arrive at our conclusion that spousal abuse is (or can be) grounds for divorce when it is already supported by the overall tenor of Scripture.

Study Questions For

Chapter 12
Spousal Abuse

1. Is adultery the only way for a man to "break faith with his wife"?
2. Define spousal abuse.
3. List and briefly describe four forms of spousal abuse. Can you think of more?
4. Does a wife have scriptural grounds to divorce her husband if he is abusive to her? Why or why not?
5. Does the New Testament plainly say, "Spousal abuse is grounds for divorce"?
6. Does the New Testament plainly say, "Spousal abuse is not grounds for divorce"?
7. What does the author mean when he says, we must look at the entirety of Scripture and ask ourselves, "What is the tenor of Scripture on this topic?"
8. What was the occasion of Paul's writing First Corinthians?
9. The author says, "I believe that spousal abuse can be grounds for divorce when the abuse is so destructive that the 'one-flesh' bond between husband and wife has been broken." Do you agree or disagree? Why?
10. According to Paul how (in what way) are husbands to love their wives?
11. Did Jesus place the church's needs before His own?
12. Can a man truly be said to be loving his wife as Christ loved the church if he is abusing her?
13. A husband is to be the shelter to which his wife can run for protection from the storm. However, when a husband abuses his wife, what does he become?
14. Why does the author say that it is curious that one reason often given for divorce and remarriage is desertion?
15. What is "constructive desertion" and what do you think of this idea?

You must make an honest woman out of her! —Julie's mom

Chapter 13

Myth Busters

Myth # 1 Making Honest Women

The young couple sat before me. Julie was pregnant, and her mom had decided that Julie and Bobby needed to get married. Julie was sixteen and Bobby was seventeen. Neither had graduated from high school. They had been dating only a few months, and now they were faced with the biggest decision of their young lives. Privately, I asked the boy, "If Julie weren't pregnant, would you still want to marry her?" Without hesitation Bobby said, "No way!"

I asked him, "So why are you getting married?" He said, "Because her mom said, *'You must make an honest woman out of her!'* So, it's the right thing to do." With all of the pastoral authority I could muster, I said, "No. It's not the right thing to do. Listen, Bobby, two wrongs do not make a right."

I encouraged them to go to counseling at a Christian pregnancy care center. I tried to explain to them what they could expect if they were to get married and raise a baby.

However, Julie's mother was a psychologically overbearing woman who was pushing very hard for the wedding. Bobby's family was "staying out of the fray" and allowing him to "make up his own mind."

I was opposed to their wedding, and I refused to perform the ceremony. Within a couple of weeks they went forward with the "blessed event" in another church and with another pastor.

Bobby dropped out of high school and got a menial job, and Julie dropped out of school and sat home in their little apartment all day. Soon, the young husband began beating his new wife. This went on for about a year, and then Julie's mother decided that they had enough of Julie being an "honest woman," and it was time for her to file for divorce.

Julie's mother spoke one of the most enduring myths of all time. If a woman (or girl) gets pregnant, the man must "make an honest woman out of her." I have no statistics on this, but I would simply guess that such marriages likely have a higher rate of divorce than normal marriages.

More Destructive Myths

As we move toward the end of this book, I am painfully aware that there are still many more issues that we could write about on the topics of marriage, divorce, and remarriage. It is impossible to deal with all of them and still make this book short enough to be manageable. However, I would like to discuss a few topics from my personal perspective as we attempt to bust some myths.

Some Myths About Love

To be sure, there are many misconceptions about love. Love is likely one of the most difficult terms or emotions to describe because so many people have so many ideas as to what it is.

Romantic Love

I think that most younger people have the idea that love is an emotion. It is what they "feel" when they are with someone who makes them happy and giddy. This sort of visceral emotion that we think is love is more likely just physical attraction or lust. This type of love is what the Greeks called *eros*. *Eros*, which is found in the *Iliad* by Homer, was a common noun meaning sexual desire. So, it is a type of love. It's what we Americans might call *Romantic Love*. That is not to say that Romantic Love cannot mature into true or deeper love; it can. I only wish to point out that there is a difference between what many people (especially younger people) think love is and what mature love is.

Some psychological researchers say that extreme Romantic Love is a form of madness.[17] Apparently, some of the same chemical reactions in the brain that people have when they are mad (insane) are also apparent in some people when they are initially thrust into Romantic Love. Who has not endured some of the symptoms of Romantic Love like heart palpitations (what some have called twiterpations), loss of appetite, mood swings, constant obsessional thinking, daydreaming, fantasizing, and sleeplessness? How many times have we heard a young person say, *"I can't live without him"* or, *"I can't live without her"*? What parents who have seen their children into adulthood have not had to deal with the silly, emotionally unstable actions of their children as a direct result of this kind of "love." Some young people have sacrificed relationships with their families and friends for Romantic Love only to have their "undying love" crash and burn a short time later. Too often people equate *love* with this head-over-heels Romantic Love.

This sort of crazy-love is not limited to the young and naïve. While many younger people do some crazy things because they are consumed with *the emotional fire* of Romantic Love, many adults have also sacrificed their families and careers for the same gut-wrenching emotion.

An adult woman left her husband for a man she had met only hours earlier. The man was on a business trip, and he came into the store where she worked. She said that when their eyes met, she "fell instantly in love with him." He asked her

---

[17] Thomas J. Scheff (Professor Emeritus of Sociology, University of California, Santa Barbara), *Attachment, Attunement, Attraction: 24 Kinds of "Love,"* "CHAPTER 4: Defining Love," August 2003, <http://www.soc.ucsb.edu/faculty/scheff/29.html> (17 August 2005). A quick check on the Internet for "Romantic Love" and "Romantic Jealousy" will bring up many more resources and scholars who say that Romantic Love is a form of madness.

to accompany him to dinner that night. Not only did she go to dinner with him, but she spent the weekend with him in his motel room. She never called her husband during that weekend, and, of course, he was worried that something terrible had happened to her. Something had. She never came home, and she didn't go into work the next morning as she was scheduled to. Her husband called the police, and the search was on.

This woman and her new "love" hid away in his motel room for the weekend. She awoke early on Monday morning only to find that the knave had skulked away before dawn. He didn't leave his real name or phone number. Lovesick and bewildered, she was unable to face her husband after such an act of betrayal. She feared talking to him and confessing what she had done. So, instead, she went directly to her lawyer and filed for a divorce. She never even gave her husband the *opportunity* to forgive her.

In the early 1990's, I became aquatinted with a pastor who had taken a church from fewer than ten people to a couple thousand in three years! This minister was married with children, and he was making a significant impact on his community for Christ. He was a gifted preacher/evangelist, and he spent hundreds of hours reaching out to the lost in his community. Many of the people in his church were first-time converts. In the fourth year, he had an affair with a married woman in his church. The affair was soon exposed, and he was removed from leadership. In spite of the valiant efforts by others in leadership, the church ultimately crumbled. The positive community impact was over, and I am sure that the devil took great delight in his destructive victory. The minister sacrificed his wife, children, and ministry for Romantic Love. Furthermore, the woman's husband and children were also betrayed and broken by the affair. It's a simple and often repeated fact that "people in love do crazy things." However, it might be better if we said, "people in Romantic Love do crazy things." Certainly Romantic Love, or some strange form thereof, had made this minister do some foolish and irresponsible things.

Please do not misunderstand me. Romantic Love is wonderful when it is tempered with maturity and wisdom. What a delight for husbands and wives to feel that "chemistry" of Romantic Love when they look at their spouses. I believe that Romantic Love is a gift from God. But, like all good things, it can be misunderstood and abused. And, Satan is all too eager to help people get a completely false idea of what true love is by promoting the visceral emotion of Romantic Love as the highest form of love. Hollywood certainly adds to this misconception as well. Movies are geared to convince us that Romantic Love is what true love is all about, and anything other than a *Romantic Love of swirling emotions* is less than what we deserve.

While Romantic Love makes some people only act silly, others who feel this torrential flow of emotion turn violent. More times than I care to count, I have heard of someone declaring, "If I can't have her, no one will." And, with that, actual murders have taken place. I've heard terrible stories of mayhem and murder, all in the name of love.

The destructive impulse is sometimes turned inward as well. Many years ago I learned that an old friend from Bible college killed himself when his girlfriend broke off their engagement. This Bible-college graduate was in his late 20's, and he had his entire life ahead of him, but he was so emotionally twisted by Romantic Love that he simply saw no other avenue. So, he committed suicide in an attempt to end his emotional turmoil.

The Grass is Not Greener on the Other Side of the Fence
Another insidious aspect of Romantic Love is "addiction." It is like a drug that makes you feel good. Any person who has experienced the euphoric ecstasy of Romantic Love wants it again, and again. Too often people get married on the basis of Romantic Love and when the "chemistry" begins to wane, they start going through "Romantic Love withdrawal," and they need another "fix." So, they begin looking for it outside their marriage. The old saying that, "The grass is always greener on the other side of the fence" is an

apt saying for the way many people feel. In reality, the proverb is sarcasm. It is intended to help us understand that the grass is *not* greener on the other side of the fence.

I was once visiting a friend's farm. He had various animals including some goats. His neighbor also had goats. He and his neighbor had erected a barbed-wire fence to separate their farms and keep their animals corralled. On that day I noted a most amusing sight. Several of my friend's goats had stuck their heads through the barbed-wire fence so they could eat the grass on the other side of the fence. However, several of the neighbor's goats had stuck their heads through the same fence and were eating the grass on his side of the fence! From where I was standing, I could see that there was plenty of lush green grass on both sides of the fence. But, those silly goats were straining through the fence, and some of them were getting cut in the process.

Too many times people do the same stupid thing. They look outside their own marriage for "greener grass." I've counseled people who divorced their spouses in search for "greener grass" who later told me that if they had it to do over, they would stay with their first spouse and make it work.

One woman told me that the "emotional chemistry" that she felt for her husband began to dissipate, and she figured that she "deserved to be happy," as she put it. So, she set her sights on a man with whom she had exchanged emotionally-charged glances. Soon, she divorced her first husband and was deliriously happy with her new, second husband. She said that she had "finally met her soul mate." There was an abundance of "Romantic Love" between them. Their fiery emotion was unquenchable . . . so she thought. Not long after they were married, reality set in. She realize that the "Romantic Love" they shared was not being sustained at the same fever pitch as earlier.

She had assumed that it was her first husband's fault when their "Romantic Love" was not as passionate as it had been. But now, it was happening all over again. Marriage, she soon discovered, was not an emotional utopia. It was, rather, a real-world relationship with another real human being who had his own share of shortcomings, weaknesses, and imperfections. Her new "knight in shining armor" was just a man, like any other man. And, ultimately, he was not much different from her first husband. Her addiction to "Romantic Love" and the self-centered notion that she "deserved to be happy" had deceived and deluded her. She went in search of "greener grass" only to find that ultimately she had come full circle. She was back to the real world of real commitments to a real man with real human imperfections and real deficiencies. Or, as the old saying goes, "warts and all."[18]

This woman simply had a wrong idea of what love was. Love is not feeling giddy all of the time. Love is not always being happy. Love is not "emotional chemistry" between two people. Love is not emotional instability and twiterpations. These things may describe Romantic Love, but mature love is more than this.

Mature Love is A Choice, Not An Emotion

Mature love is a choice, not an emotion. Mature love is a decision we make. It is a commitment to another person. No one says it better than the apostle Paul. To the Corinthian church who was not displaying true love to one another as brothers and sisters in the Lord, Paul says:

---

[18] Another lie of Hollywood is that it portrays certain men and women as perfect. These perfect people are always thoughtful and always considerate. The man is a tough and rough guy who fights all odds to save the love of his life, and he does all of this while looking extremely handsome, with perhaps one lightly bloody scratch on his face. The woman is portrayed as a no-nonsense kind of woman who can go through any and all trials, keep her sanity and do all of this while her hair and makeup never get messed up, while wearing clothes that accent her best feminine qualities. In brief, they're perfect. However, *they're not real.* Too many people are looking for these Hollywood prototypes, but there are none. Even the actors themselves who play these characters do not look and act the way that the characters they portray do. One only need to consider the extremely high divorce rate among Hollywood actors to know that they are anything but perfect.

> Love is patient, love is kind. It does not envy, it does not boast, it is not proud. It is not rude, it is not self-seeking, it is not easily angered, it keeps no record of wrongs. Love does not delight in evil but rejoices with the truth. It always protects, always trusts, always hopes, always perseveres. Love never fails (1 Corinthians 13:4-8a).

Paul does not say, Love is fun. Love is exciting. Love is giddy. Love is being happy. Love is emotional.

In fact, I would also say that love is hard work. Love is sacrifice. Instead of thinking, "I deserve to be happy," true love says "I want to make my spouse happy. I want to fulfill her or his needs." We know this is true because, as Paul says, love "is not self-seeking." Mature love is directed outward, not inward. The apostle John tells us that, "God so loved the world that he gave his one and only Son, that whoever believes in him shall not perish but have eternal life" (John 3:16). When we truly love, we give. For God so loved humankind that He *gave* His only Son.

I believe that one way for a spouse to help maintain the wonderful feelings of Romantic Love is to aggressively seek to do good to and for the other spouse. When we set our sights on our own self-seeking interests, we will always be sadly disappointed.

Some Myths About Divorce

There are many popular myths floating around about divorce. Here are just a few that I was able to track down.

1 in 2

The first myth is that often-repeated "statistic" that 1 in 2 marriages ends in divorce. It's a widely known fact that if you repeat a fib often enough, and with enough emotional gusto, people ultimately believe that it is true. This so-called divorce rate statistic is just one such often-repeated fib.

First, it appears that the *1 in 2 statistic* was only a projection by certain social scientists based on the 1970's growing divorce rate. Back then, the divorce rate reached about 41 percent, and it looked as though it would just get worse. But, it didn't. In fact, the divorce rate started dropping. So, what is the exact rate of divorce? Interestingly, I found "statistics" that ranged from 1 in 2.5 to 1 in 4; that's anywhere from 41 percent to only 25 percent. Who's right? Well, not being a social scientist nor a mathematics genius, and not having access to all of the pertinent data held in every county courthouse across America, I simply do not know. From what I could discover, however, it has never reached as high as 1 in 2.[19]

Second Marriages Are More Successful

Some say that second marriages are more successful than first marriages because people learn from their mistakes. However, it appears that the divorce rate among second marriages is higher than the divorce rate of first marriages. That is certainly not to say that second marriages never work. Many of them do. But, sadly, many people do not learn from their mistakes.

Being Unhappy is A Good Reason to Get a Divorce

I've heard people say that being unhappy in your marriage is a good reason to divorce. I cannot think of any relationship in which people are always happy. Interestingly, research has shown that people who are unhappy in their marriages tend to become more happy with time if they remain married. Divorce is not the answer for unhappiness.[20]

---

[19] Dan Hurley, "Divorce Rate: It's Not as High as You Think," *The New York Times*, April 19, 2005, <http://www.divorcereform.org/nyt05.html> (12 August 2005).

[20] Linda J. Waite, et al., "Does Divorce Make People Happy? Findings from a Study of Unhappy Marriages" Press Release, 11 July 2002, <http://www.smartmarriages.com/does.divorce.html> (17 August 2005).

All marriages have their good times and bad, and nowhere in Scripture is being unhappy considered grounds for divorce.

Divorce is Better for the Children

I was counseling a man who wanted a divorce. He said that he and his wife fought constantly. Then he said that it would be better for his children if he and his wife got a divorce because then they would not see their parents fighting all the time. Are children really better off when their parents divorce rather than seeing them in an unhappy relationship? Not at all. Some research has shown that as long as the relationship between the spouses is not violent or physically abusive, children, while negatively affected by the bad relationship, are actually better off than if their parents divorce. After speaking with the man's wife and children (none of whom wanted the divorce), I concluded that he was only using his "children's welfare" as just one more excuse to get the divorce that he so selfishly wanted. His real problems were selfishness, immaturity, and lack of commitment.

Furthermore, children of divorce themselves have a higher divorce rate than children from intact families. It's a truism that children learn from their parents, and actions speak louder than words. When children are taught by their parents' actions that marriage is of little importance or value, it should not surprise us to see them treat marriage in the same way when they are adults.[21]

Myths About Christians and Divorce Rates

There are conflicting reports as to the exact rates of divorce among Christians. Nonetheless, in what appears to be

---

[21] For more discussion and research sources for myths about divorce, see, David Popenoe, "The Top Ten Myths of Divorce: Discussion of the most common misinformation about divorce" (A publication of the National Marriage Project. © 2002) <http://marriage.rutgers.edu/Publications/pubtoptenmyths.htm> (11 August 2005).

shockingly counterintuitive, the Barna Research Group[22] interviewed 3614 adults from across America, and they found (with a margin of error of plus or minus 2 percent) that Christians in mainstream Protestant churches have a higher divorce rate than major Christian denominations like Catholics and Lutherans. Not only that, but the Barna Research Group reports that Christians have higher divorce rates than atheists and agnostics.[23]

Why is this? While people have their ideas, there are simply so many variables that no one knows for sure, but it is disturbing news to say the least.

In my research about divorce rates among Christians and non-Christians, I found what seemed to be an immediate negation of the statistics by some Christian leaders. In almost every case, Christian leaders would have a series of issues that they would "factor in" saying, in essence, it's not as bad as it appears from the statistics. Yet, these "factors" were nebulous and unsubstantiated. However, even after allowing these "factors," the reality is that born-again Christians are just as likely to divorce as are non-Christians. So, when Christian leaders say it's not as bad as it appears from the statistics, what they are actually saying is that divorce rates among Christians are no worse than that of non-Christians. This is no triumphal statement. Saying that "we're no worse than our unsaved counterparts" hardly wins the blue-ribbon prize.

---

[22] George Barna Research Group. George Barna is a born-again Christian whose company is in Ventura, CA.

[23] For more information on this topic, see, The Associated Press, "Baptists have highest divorce rate," 30 December 1999, <http://www.sullivan-county.com/bush/divorce.htm>; and The Barna Group, "Born Again Christians Just As Likely to Divorce As Are Non-Christians," 8 September 2004, <http://www.barna.org/FlexPage.aspx ?Page=BarnaUpdate &BarnaUpdateID=170> (11 August 2005); and The Barna Group, "Born Again Adults Less Likely to Co-Habit, Just as Likely to Divorce," 6 August 2001, <http://www.barna.org/FlexPage. aspx?Page=BarnaUpdate &BarnaUpdateID=95> (11 August 2005).

The sad fact is that too many Christians see divorce as just another option when they are faced with the real-life difficulties of marriage. Research groups like Barna have proven that there is an amazingly high divorce rate among Christians.

Just as bewildering to me is that many Christians downplay the statistic. But why? I would think as Christians we should decry with a prophetic voice the divorce rate among Christians as sin, and not try to massage the statistics so that it does not sound as bad as research has shown. Malachi certainly did not massage the divorce-rate statistics of his day to lessen the sin of unjustified divorce: Malachi 2:16 says, "I hate divorce." Where are God's prophets today on this issue? Let me say it: God hates treacherous, selfish, self-centered divorce!

Whether in books like this, or sermons, or in counseling, Christian leaders should be careful to deal in facts and to reflect what the Scriptures have to say about marriage, divorce, and remarriage. Of all people, Christian leaders should never trivialize marriage or divorce. We should always seek to confirm the awesome commitment that we make to another and to God. In a wedding ceremony that I recently performed, I stated this:

> When God ordained the very first marriage, the woman whom God made as Adam's companion was not taken from his head to rule over him, nor from his feet to be trampled under foot by him, but from his side that she might be his equal, from under his arm that she might receive his protection, and from near his heart that she might receive his love.

> The relation of husband and wife is most sacred when it is that of two souls with a single thought; two hearts that beat as one. It is the blending of two lives; the union of two natures. This can only be achieved when the couple understand that marriage is not a contract between two people. It is, rather, a covenant between

three people, and the third person of the covenant is God. When a couple is joined in holy matrimony, they are joined by God, and they make their vows to each other and to God. Vows to one another and to God are not promises that one should enter into lightly.

However, even though Christians often speak of the permanency of marriage and the sin of divorce, mainstream Protestant Christians are divorcing at a higher rate than our liberal and atheistic counterparts! This is simply astounding.

While Christians should never employ unscriptural and legalistic tactics to prevent scripturally justifiable divorce and remarriage, neither should Christians twist God's Holy Word to accommodate their personal, self-centered desire to divorce.

The 1 in 1,152 Myth

There is a new myth that is now floating around. Perhaps we can nip it in the bud before it gets too well worn. This myth says that if a Christian couple will pray together for one to two minutes a day, their divorce rate shifts from 1 in 2 to 1 in 1,152.

Where does this statistic come from? So far, I have not been able to find anyone who will own up to the origin of this statistic. One Internet web page that repeated this "statistic" as if it were real said that a "secular organization" had made this discovery.

However, let the science of this ratio sink down into your mind for a moment. The first error, as mentioned above, is that the divorce rate is not 1 in 2. Next, to get a 1 in 1,152 ratio, the sheer size of the number of the test subjects would be phenomenal in social research. If this questionable statistic had even stated daily prayer caused the divorce rate to shift from 1 in 2 to 1 in 5, it would still be incredible. Now, anytime someone makes these kinds of claims, there are two areas that have to come into play: Mathematics and Social Science. So, I contacted a few experts in these two fields.

First, let's look at mathematics. A scientifically substantiated survey will talk in ratios with a "margin of error." This 1 in 1,152 "statistic" mentions no such margin of error. So, I asked Ed Pegg Jr. to estimate the sheer mathematics of such a ratio. What I asked him specifically was this: "Just out of curiosity, what number of test subjects would it take to even possibly come up with this ratio?" His response is telling. He said,

> For odds that small, and that *exact*, it would be a huge sample size. For odds of "about 1 in 1000," then 1000 or 2000 people. Note that no margin or error is given, and margin of error is required in order to bound the sample size. To be sure of this exact figure, it would be more like 100,000, or more.[24]

Note that he says, "For odds of '*about* 1 in 1000,' then 1000 or 2000 people (emphasis mine). The "about," here is the margin of error. But, with no margin of error in the 1 in 1,152 ratio, they would need 100,000, or more test subjects!

Now, it seems to me that if anyone or any organization of any reputation had done a survey this colossal on such a hot topic as divorce, this statistic would not be hard to find. It would be out there on the internet by the thousands.

Looking up Barna's research on divorce led me to more than 34,800 hits on Google.com. However, when I did a similar search for the 1 in 1,152 statistics, I found only three links (and two of them were to the same article that repeated the statistic as if it were true). None of the links provided evidence; they just repeated this highly dubious statistic. One of the web sites stated, "Recently a secular organization was attempting to determine why the divorce rate is so high.

---

[24] Ed Pegg Jr. is the webmaster for mathpuzzle.com. He works at Wolfram Research, Inc. as an associate editor of *MathWorld*, and as administrator of the Mathematica Information Center. E-mail of 12 Aug 2005, on file.

Surprisingly, they discovered that the divorce rate among couples who prayed together was 1 in 1,152."[25]

"Surprisingly, they discovered"? How does one simply "stumble" upon such a truth? This makes it sound like they accidentally "discovered" this 1 in 1,152 statistic. The other web site said, " . . . the statistics are dramatic when there's a strong faith-based family. 'Today 1 in 2 marriages fail. But if a man prays and communicates his heart with his wife, only 1 in 1,152 marriages fail!' says Shiloh."[26]

In reality we have no idea who this "secular organization" is. No organization (secular or otherwise) has come forward to state that this was their "discovery." There's not even a mention of who did this research. This is not evidence. It is one of those often-repeated fibs by likely well-meaning but misled Christians. It is one of those urban myths that gets passed around, and the lack of evidence for such a statement is exactly the sort of thing that the world uses to discredit "Christian research," and, rightly so if Christians uncritically repeat (or forward by e-mail) these things as though they were facts without having evidence for support.

Next, I asked a social scientist for his thoughts on this supposed survey. In short, he said that this sort of "ill-founded claim" about the ability of religious practices to shift people to a lesser divorce rate brings us "into the realm of Magic Thinking where in general we should not be in the 21st Century."[27]

---

[25] http://66.102.7.104/search?q=cache:zbbZxyiWCQsJ: www. wisecounselonline.com/index2.php%3Foption%3Dcontent%26do_pdf%3 D1%26id%3D31+%221+in+1,152%22+divorce&hl=en&ie=UTF-8 (12 August 2005).

[26] Craig R. Smith, "Healing fatherlessness" WorldNetDaily.com June 13, 2005 <http://www.worldnetdaily.com/news/article.asp? ARTICLE_ID=44744> (22 August 2005).

[27] Craig McKie, Department of Sociology and Anthropology, Carleton University, Ottawa, Ontario. E-mail of 16 Aug 2005, on file.

I agree, and I would add that I think it is simply a case of wishful thinking and desire-beliefs for people to uncritically believe that 1 to 2 minutes of prayer time together each day will lift their ratio of divorce from 1 in 2 (which was shown above as being inaccurate as well) to 1 in 1,152.

Inconsistent Premise

Even the premise of this so-called "research" is not consistent. From one person, I heard it this way:

> The rule of thumb is that 1 out of every 2 marriages end in divorce, in the church and out of the church. HOWEVER, if a couple prays together every day . . . [just] 1 or 2 minutes of prayer with a husband and his wife that number changes from 1 out of 2 marriages to 1 out of 1,152 marriages that end in divorce.[28]

Someone else stated it as:

> Recently a secular organization was attempting to determine why the divorce rate is so high. Surprisingly, they discovered that the divorce rate among couples who prayed together was 1 in 1,152.[29]

And, yet another has it:

> . . . the statistics are dramatic when there's a strong faith-based family. 'Today 1 in 2 marriages fail. But if a man prays and communicates his heart with his wife, only 1 in 1,152 marriages fail!' says Shiloh.[30]

[28] Personal e-mail from a friend. E-mail on file, 10 August 2005.

[29] http://66.102.7.104/search?q=cache:zbbZxyiWCQsJ: www. wisecounselonline.com/index2.php%3Foption%3Dcontent%26do_pdf%3 D1%26id%3D31+%221+in+1,152%22+divorce&hl=en&ie=UTF-8 (12 August 2005).

[30] Craig R. Smith, "Healing fatherlessness" (22 August 2005).

Well, which is it? Is it the 1 to 2 minutes of prayer that makes the change? Is it just praying together but not precisely 1 to 2 minutes a day? Or, is it as the third one has it if a man prays and communicates his heart with his wife the odds jump to 1 in 1,152? One says that the husband and wife must pray together for 1 to 2 minutes a day. The next says that they just must pray together, but it does not say how often or how much. Finally, the last one says that they need to pray together, and the man needs to share his heart with his wife (but what that is exactly is not explained); again, it does not say how often they should pray together or how much.

However, surveys of scientific value will be precise in their premise and what it is that they are seeking to learn from the survey subjects.

Furthermore, simple logic seems to destroy this myth of 1 in 1,152. Think of it for just a moment: George Barna has shown (scientifically with real statistics and data) that Christians have a higher divorce rate than do non-Christians. Are we really expected to believe that none of these Christian couples who are divorcing prayed together? Having been a pastor for 20 years and a counselor for longer than that, I have seen Christian couples who prayed together, who shared their hearts with each other, who still end up in divorce court.

Divorce Rate Surveys Are About What Happened

Last, these sorts of surveys are about "what happened," not about what will happen. Are we really expected to believe that an unnamed organization "out there somewhere" tracked about 100,000 people for their entire lives, and checked on their daily prayer activities, to show that they never divorced? To prove this 1 in 1,152 ratio, the researchers would have had to track all of the test subjects throughout their entire lives to see if they ever got divorced. A research project this colossal would likely have cost millions of dollars, and it would have extended over a period of as many as 70 years. Quite a feat! Yet no one has come forward to claim to be the "the secular organization" who did this fantastic, gargantuan and decades-long study. Furthermore, of those who have this "statistic" on their web sites, none of them returned my e-mails or phone calls asking for verification of their sources.

The simple fact, however, is that this shift of 1 in 2 to 1 in 1,152 because of 1 to 2 minutes of daily spousal prayer is simply an urban myth (and wishful thinking).

Spousal Prayer is Good

Now, before I am misunderstood, let me state emphatically that I think a daily spousal prayer time is a good thing. It is altogether likely that all married Christians should spend more time praying with their spouses, and I do believe that men should share their hearts with their wives, and vice versa. A friend who is a *Certified Marriage Specialist* wrote to me on this issue and said, "I would confidently say that there are more Christian couples who never pray together than those who pray daily and those who sometimes pray together combined."[31]

Obviously Christian couples should spend time praying together. My contention is simply that spousal prayer time is not a "magic formula" that will lift you to a 1 in 1,152 chance of divorce. In brief, there is no "magic pill" or "incantation" or "secret formula" that when employed increases your chances of marital longevity.

In fact, the secret to a long, happy marriage is no secret at all. It is obvious. The necessary things are uncompromising commitment, self-sacrificing love, selflessness, and commitment. Paul said it well when he said:

> Love is patient, love is kind. It does not envy, it does not boast, it is not proud. It is not rude, it is not self-seeking, it is not easily angered, it keeps no record of wrongs. Love does not delight in evil but rejoices with the truth. It always protects, always trusts, always hopes, always perseveres. Love never fails (1 Corinthians 13:4-

---

[31] Denny Nissley, *Certified Marriage Specialist*, personal e-mail on file, 23 Aug 2005.

8a).

We must remember that Christians, by definition, are "believers." Far too often, however, Christians too easily believe what they are told, especially if it is coming from a man standing on a platform, or, nowadays, from a slick Christian web site. Solomon says, "Only simpletons believe everything they are told! The prudent carefully consider their steps" (New Living Translation, Proverbs 14:15). Christians must use wise discernment. Things that sound too good to be true usually are. This "pray one to two minutes a day with your spouse and lift your divorce rate from 1 in 2 to 1 in 1,152," is simply a myth.

Study Questions For

Chapter 13
Myth Busters

1. The author says that "Love is likely one of the most difficult terms or emotions to describe." Why is this so?

2. What does the author mean by the term "Romantic Love"?

3. Is "Romantic Love" limited to the young and naïve?

4. What sorts of things have adults sacrificed for illicit "Romantic Love"?

5. When is Romantic Love wonderful?

6. How do you think that Hollywood adds to the misconception that Romantic Love is true love, and anything else is less than we deserve?

7. Have people in Romantic Love ever turned violent? How?

8. What is the point of the old saying that, "The grass is always greener on the other side of the fence"? And, how does it relate to the issue of divorce and remarriage?

9. The author says that "Mature love is a choice. It is a decision we make. It is a commitment to another person." Do you agree with this? Why or why not?

10. To the Corinthian church the apostle Paul says, "Love is not self-seeking." What does he mean by this?

11. What is one way that the author believes a person can help maintain the wonderful feelings of Romantic Love for his/her spouse?

12. When we set our sights on our own self-seeking interests, what will be the outcome?

13. Why do some say that second marriages are more successful than first marriages?

14. Is it a statistical fact that second marriages never last?

15. Is being unhappy in your marriage a good reason to divorce?

16. Do you think that divorce is better for children than allowing them to see their parents fighting? Why or why not?

17. What are the statistical facts about Christians and divorce rates?

18. When faced with the statistical facts about Christians and divorce rates, what is the best thing that Christian leaders can do?

19. What should Christians decry with a prophetic voice?

20. Should Christians employ unscriptural and legalistic tactics to prevent scripturally justifiable divorce and remarriage?

21. Should Christians twist God's Word to accommodate their personal, self-centered desire to divorce?

22. What does the author say are the three necessary things for a long, happy marriage?

23. Why does the author say that this *"pray one to two minutes a day with your spouse and lift your divorce rate from 1 in 2 to 1 in 1,152,"* is simply a myth?

*A chicken and pig were trying to figure out what they could
do to give something to their master who had been very
good to them. The chicken said, "I know. Tomorrow
for breakfast, we'll give him bacon and eggs."
The pig replied, "Oh, I don't think so.
For you that's just an involvement;
for me it's a commitment."*

Chapter 14

Commitment and Involvement

I was 13 years old, and my girlfriend lived only a few blocks from my home. I'd walk her home from school, and often walk or ride my bicycle to her house on weekends.

As silly as this may sound to adults, back then I thought that I was in love with her and that she was the girl I was going to marry.

Then, her family moved across town, and it made my "commute" much more difficult. She now lived about five miles from my home! It was an unpleasant and seemingly arduous bike ride, and even a longer walk.

At that time there was a popular love song with lyrics that said something like, "I'd climb the highest mountain and swim the deepest sea just to be near you." One day as my girlfriend and I sat on her front porch (aka stoop), we were listening to the radio and that love song came on. Together we listened to those words of commitment and when the song ended, I said, "You know that's how I feel about you. I'd climb the highest mountain and swim the deepest sea just to be near you." She smiled broadly, and we just sat there for a few moments holding hands.

Then she said, "Oh, by the way, I'll be home all day this Saturday. You want to come over?"

And I said, "Sure, if it doesn't rain."

As obviously funny as that sounds now, neither of us noted the irony then. No one expects 13-year-olds to be ready for lifetime marriage commitments, but I have seen couples who were about to get married who were not much more committed than I was at 13.

Fair-Weather Commitment

We've all heard of the term, a "fair-weather friend." That's a friend who supports others only when it is easy and convenient to do so. It is a person who is dependable only in the good times but not in times of trouble.

Without consciously thinking of it, some people view commitment in precisely this same way. It is what I call a "fair-weather commitment."

A very good example of this happened in a premarital counseling session I had with one young couple. I asked the them if they were ready to commit to each other for life. Without hesitation, they both said "yes" at the same time. So, I asked them to tell me what they thought commitment meant.

Each of them had a vague idea of the meaning of the word. The young man said, "Commitment is cool as long as things are good between the husband and wife." I was concerned that he really had no genuine idea of what the term meant. Without even knowing it, his idea of commitment was a "fair-weather commitment." Since he was a native of the Pacific Northwest and was wearing a Seattle Seahawks jacket, I asked him who his favorite professional football team was. "The Seattle Seahawks!" he blurted out; "They're *my* team!"

So, I asked him how many Super Bowl games the Hawks had won. "None," was his reply. "Well, how may Super Bowl games have they at least played in?" I asked. He nervously smiled and said "none." So, I asked, "Have they ever been to the playoffs?" "Yeah, some," he said. But, you're still committed to them?" I asked. "Absolutely," he said.

So I said, "Well, didn't you just say that 'commitment is cool as long as things are good between the husband and wife.'"? Slowly he said, "y-e-a-h." Then I asked him, "What would it take for you to shift and become a fan of another pro team?"

"Ain't going to happen," he responded, "like I said, the Hawks are *my* team." "So, you're not a fair-weather fan of the Seahawks; you're with them through thick and thin?" I asked. "Absolutely," was his reply.

Then I said, "So, let me get this straight; you're more committed to your football team even when they don't win games than you plan to be with your wife?"

He just sat there, and for a moment I let this concept sink down into his mind. Then, I said, "Are you willing to commit yourself to this woman as much as you have committed yourself to the Seahawks? Win, lose, or draw, are you ready to be her biggest fan for the rest of your life, even if this marriage never makes it to the *marriage Super Bowl*, or never even makes it to the *playoffs?*"

I believe that it was at that moment that this young man first began to understand what it meant to be committed to a wife for life.

Commitment An Essential Ingredient

Commitment is an essential ingredient in mature love and a solid marriage. Like the word love itself, the word commitment is often misunderstood because people have different ideas as to what it means. The word commitment means the act of binding one's self to a person or a course of action until that person has died or that course of action is complete. Anything short of that is not commitment. It may be "involvement," but it is not a commitment.

Too many people, both men and women, have a "fair-weather commitment," something like, "I am committed to this person or course of action as long as it is good for me." This sort of "commitment" really means nothing more than involvement.

Throughout our lives, we all become involved with others. People we work with, neighbors, and even friends. But, over the years, we have different coworkers, different neighbors, and even different friends. While I was deeply involved with some of my coworkers, neighbors, and friends of 15 years ago, today I have many different coworkers, neighbors, and friends with whom I am deeply involved.

Funny thing, however, during those years, I never got a new set of parents or a new set of siblings. Likewise, during those years I never got a new spouse. Like parents or siblings, a spouse is for your lifetime. Anything short of this is not commitment. If a spouse commits adultery, or commits spousal abuse, or deserts the other, or divorces the other, it shows that the person simply was not committed. The person may have been maritally involved, but he or she was simply not truly committed.

This confusion about commitment and involvement is all too often seen in marriages. The young man who said, "Commitment is cool as long as things are good between the husband and wife," was really echoing what many believe but have never articulated. It describes a "fair-weather commitment," or involvement. In premarital counseling, couples talk about commitment and the counselor might ask if the two are willing to commit to one another for life. And, generally without hesitation, the couple affirm that they are ready to do so. However, what they are often really saying is that as long as things go well, they'll be maritally involved with each other.

Commitment, however, means you are making a vow for life, no matter how good or how bad it gets, and only death can break the vow.

The Jesus Commitment

I remember as a young Christian coming to the realization of Jesus' commitment to me as a sinner when I came across this passage of Scripture: "For there is one God and one mediator between God and men, the man Christ Jesus" (1 Timothy 2:5). Keep in mind that this passage was written by Paul in about A.D. 62 or 63. This is well after Christ came to earth, died, rose, and ascended to heaven.

You see, even after Jesus died, rose from the dead, and returned to heaven, He was still "the *man* Christ Jesus." When Jesus took on human flesh, He did so for all eternity. While Jesus always has been and always shall be 100% God, at His incarnation, He took on humanity, so He is now also 100% human. Jesus is not half God and half man. He did not stop being God when He came to earth, and He did not stop being human when He returned to heaven. John 1:14b says, "The Word [i.e., Jesus] became flesh and made his dwelling among us." He "became flesh." And, He committed to remain in that flesh (though now glorified due to His resurrection) for all eternity. This is a breathtaking commitment! The second person of the eternal God taking on human flesh for all eternity. In some of the false, world religions that I have studied, their so-called gods only become involved with humanity. But the one and only true God made an eternal commitment to humanity. Paul describes it like this in Philippians:

> Your attitude should be the same as that of Christ Jesus: Who, being in very nature God, did not consider equality with God something to be grasped, but made himself nothing, taking the very nature of a servant, being made in human likeness. And being found in appearance as a man, he humbled himself and became obedient to death—even death on a cross! (Philippians 2:5-8)

Jesus did not just get involved with us. He made a commitment to us, an eternal commitment.

Another good example of the concept of involvement versus commitment is that of being a soldier. In all wars there are soldiers who face mortal danger, and still they advance and fight. Also, in all wars there are some who go AWOL (absent without leave). I have always found it awe-inspiring that soldiers on the front lines of combat march directly into harm's way knowing that a large number of them will never return, and still they march. This is commitment. For those who turn tail and run, they were never committed; they were only involved. When the going got tough, they clearly showed that they were not committed soldiers.

Not Ready to Commit? Don't Get Married

A pastor was doing premarital counseling with a young couple, and he talked with the couple at length about the true concept of commitment.

After a few sessions, the man told the pastor that he simply had no idea that he was expected to commit himself to that degree. The pastor told him that there are no degrees of commitment. Either you are committed or you are not. The pastor told him that if he was not 100% committed, then he was only involved, and marriage does not call one to be involved, it calls one to be committed. Remember, when you make your vows of marriage, he reminded him, you are making a commitment to your spouse and to God. In the marriage vows, we do not say, "I promise to be involved with this person." Likewise, when I have done marriage ceremonies in the past, I had the men make this vow:

> I, [man's name], take you [woman's name], to be my lawfully wedded wife, to have and to hold from this day forward, for better for worse, for richer for poorer, in sickness and in health, to love and to cherish till death shall part us, and to you and you alone, I pledge my love.

Then, I reverse it and had the women make the same vow to their husbands. This is not a simple involvement. This is a till-death-shall-part-us commitment made to one another and to God.

The young man told the pastor that he was simply not ready to make that kind of a commitment. To this the pastor said, "I believe that if two people are not ready to truly and totally commit to one another, then they should not get married." Then, the man called off the wedding. The would-be bride, however, was livid, and she blamed the pastor for scaring her fiancé away. While certainly the woman had every right to be saddened by the event, she should have recognized that the pastor only uncovered at that time a problem that would have surfaced later after marriage. Better before the marriage to know where each person stands on the issue of commitment than after the marriage.

A longtime friend of mind told me that when he was a young man of 20, he liked two Christian women, and he thought that either of them would be a good wife. So, he asked each of them what they thought of marriage and commitment. One of them said, "Well, I just figure that if it doesn't work out, we can always get a divorce." He married the other woman. Today, in their 60's, they are thoroughly enjoying their grandchildren.

Study Questions For

Chapter 14
Commitment and Involvement

1. How would you define the difference between Commitment and Involvement?
2. Define "Fair-Weather Commitment."
3. How did the author use the concept of being a fan of a professional football team help a young man understand the meaning of commitment?
4. Define the word commitment.
5. How does the author use the Incarnation of Jesus as an example of commitment?
6. How does the author use the concept of being a soldier as an example of commitment?
7. Are there degrees of commitment? Why or why not?
8. In this chapter, the author speaks of a pastor who said, "I believe that if two people are not ready to truly and totally commit to one another, then they should not get married." Do you agree with this pastor? Why or why not?

A sound marriage is not based on complete frankness;
it is based on a sensible reticence.—Morris L. Ernst

Chapter 15

A Gem of Marriage Wisdom

My wife and I were enjoying the wedding reception. A nice young couple had just gotten married, and a book was being passed around. The book contained many blank pages, and the guests were asked to contribute "Gems of Marriage Wisdom." The key question was this: ***What one piece of advice would you give to the new bride and groom?***

Bite Your Tongue

My wife wrote perhaps the greatest piece of wisdom that anyone that day had penned. She wrote: "Learn to bite your tongue." Morris L. Ernst said the same thing in the quote that begins this chapter: "A sound marriage is not based on complete frankness; it is based on a sensible reticence."

There are many ingredients that go into making a good marriage, and I have learned one very valuable ingredient from my wife: Do not speak every thought that comes into your mind, especially when you are angry. In short, "Learn to bite your tongue." Words spoken in anger can never be retrieved.

I counseled a young couple who were screaming *DIVORCE* at one another. Once I was able to calm them down, we began to backtrack to find out what had started this conflagration. "Well, she started it!" the man said. "No I didn't," she retaliated, "You started it when you said . . ." and on it went. As we kept backtracking, I noted that they were both more and more vague about exactly what it was that had started it all to begin with. Ultimately, we backed up enough to discover that neither one remembered what had originated the fight! So, I asked them, "Do you really wish to end your marriage on an issue that neither of you can even remember?" I then asked each of them, "How big of a deal could it possibly have been if you can't even remember what started it?" Finally, they both just laughed at the silliness of the entire thing.

How much better would it have been if the wife or the husband (or both!) would have simply kept quiet about the small issue at the beginning and let it go? There would never have been this long and drawn out fight, and neither one of them would have been screaming about going to divorce court.

Let it Go

In part two of my wife's advice, after she said, "Learn to bite your tongue," she said, "and let it go." As I said above, there are many ingredients that go into making a good marriage, but if I can give only one small gem of wisdom to couples, young and old, it is my wife's good counsel: "Learn to bite your tongue, and let it go." You will find that if you do this, it is better than verbally retaliating.

Solomon said it this way: "A gentle answer turns away wrath, but a harsh word stirs up anger. The tongue of the wise commends knowledge, but the mouth of the fool gushes folly" (Proverbs 15:1-2).

Study Questions For

Chapter 15
Learn To Bite Your Tongue

1. What is another way of saying, "A sound marriage is not based on complete frankness; it is based on a sensible reticence"?
2. What was the one piece of advice the author's wife gave to the new bride and groom?
3. What was part two of her advice?
4. What does Proverbs 15:1-2 say?

To finish a work? To finish a picture? What nonsense! To
finish it means to be through with it, to kill it, to rid it of its
soul, to give it its final blow the coup de grâce for the
painter as well as for the picture.—Pablo Picasso

Chapter 16

A Review and Summation

In the quote above, Picasso passionately argues that an artist never really finishes a work. Another artist, whose name escapes me now, once said something like, *"I never complete a sculpture. I abandon it."*

I believe I understand their sentiment. Though I have come to the end of this book, I do not feel like it is complete. Each time I review its pages, I think of more topics and issues that can (and should) be dealt with. In other words, I do not feel "finished."

However, with the unknown artist, I must now lay down my "hammer and chisel" and *abandon* this work.

I hope that I have sculpted a clear image of *A Biblical View of Marriage, Divorce & Remarriage.*

The remaining pages of this book are a quick review and summation of the pertinent principles from the earlier chapters.

Forbidding or Regulating?

You do not regulate something that you forbid. You just forbid it. Yet, all throughout the Bible, God regulates divorce and remarriage. Thus, it is obvious that He does not simply forbid divorce and remarriage. God regulated divorce and remarriage through the law of Moses, through the teachings of Jesus, and through the teachings of His apostle, Paul.

Second Class Citizens?

We must be careful not to treat people who have been divorced and remarried as second-class citizens in the kingdom of God. We should remember two things: First, the old saying, "There but by the grace of God go I." No one is above the ravages and destruction of sin. And, Solomon tells us that "Pride goes before destruction, a haughty spirit before a fall" (Proverbs 16:18). The prophet Micah tells us how we are to be; "He has showed you, O man, what is good. And what does the LORD require of you? To act justly and to love mercy and to walk humbly with your God" (6:8). When Christians look down on other Christians and think that they themselves are above reproach, they have forgotten Solomon's and Micah's words of warnings and imperatives. Also, Paul says, "Brothers, if someone is caught in a sin, you who are spiritual should restore him gently. But watch yourself, *or you also may be tempted*" (emphasis mine, Galatians 6:1). Second, we should not forget that God Himself is a divorcé (Jeremiah 3:8a; Isaiah 50:1).

The Marriage Covenant

According to the Bible, marriage is an institution created and sanctified by God. The biblical model of marriage is that of a covenant. A covenant is between the two marriage partners and a Third Person, God. In the covenant of marriage, God actually joins the couple together and makes them one, and to break the marriage covenant is to sin not only against the spouse but also against God Himself.

God designed marriage to be a lifetime commitment. And, finally, the marriage relationship is to be the highest of human relationships, eclipsing even that of parent and child.

I Hate Divorce

While we know that God says plainly, "I hate divorce" (Malachi 2:16), we must understand that God does not hate every divorce, every time, in the same way. He hates the selfish and self-centered divorce that has no justifiable (biblical) reason as was the case in Malachi's day.

No Divorce For Christians

For *Christian couples,* Paul says that there is to be no divorce. Period. But, if a Christian couple does divorce, both the husband and the wife are to remain single allowing for the possibility of reconciliation. There is no option for divorced Christians to remarry, unless of course they remarry each other.

Even in mixed-marriages, the believer is not to initiate a divorce. If a believer is married to an unbeliever and the unbeliever is content to remain in the marriage, then the Christian is obligated by the covenant of marriage to remain married to the unbeliever.

If The Unbeliever Wants A Divorce

Paul says that a Christian may allow an unbelieving partner to get a divorce. If the unbelieving spouse decides to leave and thus end the marriage, the believing partner may let him/her go. Note well that the believer does not "send the spouse away," but rather the unbeliever chooses to separate from (divorce) the believer. "A believing man or woman is not bound in such circumstances" (1 Corinthians 7:15b).

Desire-Beliefs

Too often people have allowed their desire-beliefs to dictate their theology about the topics of divorce and remarriage. However, we should allow only the Bible to dictate our beliefs. Jesus made clear a situation when it is permissible for a believer to actually initiate a divorce. Jesus states that one may divorce one's spouse for fornication (Matthew 5:32; 19:9, KJV). The word *fornication* is simply sexual, marital unfaithfulness, i.e., adultery.

Remarriage Restrictions
Deuteronomy 24:1-4 says that if a divorced woman remarries another man and the second husband dies or divorces her, she cannot get remarried to her first husband.

It is simply unbiblical to teach that if one is divorced and remarried and wants to become right with God, then he/she must divorce the second partner and remarry the first partner. There is nothing in Scripture that would lead one to this idea (in fact, Deuteronomy 24:1-4 says just the opposite).

Jesus forbids the remarriage of persons who have divorced without just cause (Matthew 5:32; 19:9; Mark 10:11, 12; Luke 16:18).

Paul states that if a Christian couple does get a divorce, they are to remain single, not remarrying. This leaves open an opportunity and availability for a reconciliation between them (1 Corinthians 7:10-11).

Remarriage Options
When a spouse has committed adultery, the other spouse is free from the marriage covenant which has been broken because of the adultery. The exception clause (in Matthew 5:32 and 19:9) refers not only to the divorce aspect of the passage, but it refers to the remarriage aspect as well.

Paul likewise gives a remarriage option: "Yet if the unbelieving one leaves, let him leave. The brother or sister is not under bondage in such cases, but God has called us to peace" (1 Corinthians 7:15). Thus, the person who has been divorced by the nonbeliever is free both from the marriage covenant and free to remarry.

An Unrepentant Continual State of Adultery?
The word fornication (Greek: *porneia*) in the exception clause is not referring to an unrepentant, continual state of

adultery. It is absurd to suggest that a continual state must be in effect for *porneia* to be *porneia*. One needed to commit adultery only one time under the Old Testament law before he or she was put to death by stoning.

Do Not Accept One Passage At The Exclusion of Another

We are not to accept one passage at the exclusion of another, but we must harmonize them. We must shift from Paul's instructions to Jesus' instructions if the ongoing circumstances change. For the Christian couple, the absolute truth of God is that there is to be no divorce, but if they do divorce, they are to remain single allowing for a possible reconciliation (1 Corinthians 7:10-11). However, if one spouse commits adultery during that time of separation, the absolute truth of God, given to us by Jesus, is that the innocent party may remarry (Matthew 5:32; 19:9). Thus, Christian ethics allows the circumstances to reveal which absolute truth of God we are to follow.

The Husband of One Wife

Paul's statement that an overseer (pastor) must be the husband of one wife is interpreted by various people and churches to mean different things. However, there is nothing in the context or in the very words themselves to lead one to conclude that this means the overseer must not have been divorced and remarried. Paul is most likely referring to the issue of monogamy over polygamy.

Contrary to some popular teachings, polygamy was indeed an issue in New Testament times, and for many years thereafter. As in the Old Testament, God wants His leaders to be monogamous. Thus, only a man who was "the husband of one wife," i.e., monogamous, could serve as a pastor (overseer, elder).

Going Beyond The Holiness of God

Some Christians today add extra measures of legalism that God never intended. When we set our own requirements and restrictions, we move from His righteousness to *self-*

righteousness. We should find out what God actually said and live by His rules. This includes God's rules and regulations concerning divorce and remarriage.

Spousal Abuse

It is likely that we can all think of scenarios that would be so bad or injurious to the wife that we would believe that it is grounds for divorce. Thus, the question is not, "Is spousal abuse grounds for divorce?" The question is, "How bad does the abuse have to be before a woman has grounds for divorce?"

Husbands are to love their wives as Christ loved the church, *and Christ died for the church.* Can a man truly be loving his wife as Christ loved the church if he is abusing her?

Abuse that would justify divorce must break the one-flesh bond between husband and wife.

Desertion as Grounds for Divorce

While I do see true desertion as grounds for divorce and remarriage, I would not attempt to make Paul's words in 1 Corinthians 7:15 say something that he did not intend. It is better to see the concept of desertion in the overall tenor of Scripture and make one's determination on that basis, rather than manipulating a passage of Scripture to arrive at that conclusion.

The Myths

When we misunderstand what love is, thinking that it is an emotional feeling instead of a solid, mature decision, we will be unprepared to maintain a lifelong commitment to those we claim to love. Some have confused Romantic Love with mature love, and in so doing they have simply misunderstood love altogether. Romantic Love may be thought of as the beginnings of mature love, but if the love does not grow and mature, it will either simply burn out or degenerate into a destructive emotion.

Divorce Rates

While some argue over the exact divorce rates between Christians and non-Christians, it seems obvious to any objective viewer that the divorce rate among Christians is simply astounding. Christian leaders should spend more time preaching and teaching the truth of God's Word on the topic of divorce than attempting to make the problem of a high divorce rate seem less problematic. Let's face it: *we have a problem with divorce in the church.* Let's not try to justify or deny it; let's get back to the Word of God and attempt to correct it.

Commitment and Involvement

Commitment is an essential ingredient in mature love and a solid marriage. It means the act of binding one's self to a person or a course of action until that person has died or that course of action is complete. Anything short of that is not commitment. It may be "involvement," but it is not a commitment. Marriage does not call one to be involved, it calls one to be committed. When you make your vows of marriage, you are making a commitment to your spouse and to God.

A Gem of Marriage Wisdom

If I could give only one small gem of wisdom to couples, it is my wife's good counsel: "Learn to bite your tongue, and let it go." You will find that if you do this, it is better than verbally retaliating. "A gentle answer turns away wrath, but a harsh word stirs up anger. The tongue of the wise commends knowledge, but the mouth of the fool gushes folly" (Proverbs 15:1-2).

Something Happened On The Way To "Happily Ever After"
A Biblical View of Marriage, Divorce & Remarriage

Final Study Questions

1. Does God hate divorce?
2. Does God hate all divorce?
3. If you said yes to the last question, qualify your answer by describing at least three kinds of divorce and why God hates them all equally. If you said no, explain why God does not hate all divorce.
4. Is God a divorcé? (Give Scripture)
5. You do not _____ something you forbid.
6. Since God regulated divorce through His Old Testament laws, what does that tell you?
7. Was the school of Hillel conservative or liberal?
8. Was the school of Shammai conservative or liberal?
9. What is an accepted translation of *erwat debar*?
10. More difficult than translating *erwat debar* is understanding what is meant by it. Why does the author say that *erwat debar* probably does not mean adultery?
11. Why did Moses allow a man to give his wife a certificate of divorce?
12. Does Paul say that two Christians can divorce?
13. Explain what Paul does say about Christians and divorce.
14. In a mixed marriage, i.e., believer/unbeliever, can the believer initiate the divorce if the unbeliever doesn't want the divorce?
15. In a mixed marriage, if the unbeliever initiates the divorce, is the believer free to remarry?
16. Jesus referred to an acceptable reason for a Christian to initiate a divorce. What was it?
17. Define the word *fornication*, in modern-day, American English usage, and also in 17th century British English.
18. According to *Webster's Seventh New Collegiate*

Dictionary that the author quoted earlier in this book, how many years ago in American culture did the meaning of the word *fornication* include adultery?

19. What is the Greek word that the English KJV translates as fornication?

20. What is the meaning of the Greek word *porneia*?

21. Why in modern American speech are the English translations *New International Version*, the *New American Standard*, and the *New King James Version* better in their translation of the Greek word *porneia* than the *King James Version*?

22. What are the two passages in which Jesus says that one can initiate divorce because of adultery?

23. In what situation did Moses say that a man could not remarry a former spouse? Might there be an exception to Moses' restriction? If so, what and why?

24. Can Christians who have divorced for reasons of incompatibility alone remarry other people?

25. What is the exception clause, and who is the one who gave it?

26. Does the exception clause extend to remarriage? Why or why not?

27. In what situation does Paul say that a person can remarry after a divorce?

28. Should a person who is divorced and remarried, divorce his/her second spouse and return to the first spouse in an effort to make things right? Why or why not?

29. What are the four interpretations of the passage in 1 Timothy 3:2 where Paul says that the pastor should be "the husband of one wife"? And, which do you think is correct and why?

30. Which of the four interpretations of "the husband of one wife" in 1 Timothy 3:2 do you believe is correct, and why?

31. Is *porneia* a continual state of unrepentant sexual immorality? Explain your answer.

32. You cannot accept one verse of Scripture to the _____ of another.

33. If we make up and impose restrictions that go beyond what Christ says, we move from ___ _____ to ___ _____.

34. Should a Christian stay in a mixed marriage, i.e., believer/unbeliever? Explain your answer.

35. What do you think is God's highest ideal when there has been adultery in a marriage? Why?

36. Some people teach that there is never any reason for divorce and remarriage. Give at least two examples from the Scripture showing that there are grounds for divorce and remarriage.

37. In the Old Testament, who was forbidden to have polygamous marriages, and what might be the New Testament counterpart to this restriction?

38. What makes a marriage a covenant and not just a contract?

39. Is it true that Jesus commanded a person to divorce his/her spouse if the spouse had committed adultery?

40. How many times did one have to commit adultery in the Old Testament before he/she was stoned to death and how does that fact relate to the exception clause of the New Testament?

41. Pretend that you are a counselor. A women comes to you and says that her husband committed adultery, but he has repented and asked her for forgiveness. Also, he has broken off the relationship with the other woman. She is not sure if she can truly get over the emotional pain of the betrayal or not, but she wants to know what her options are. What is your counsel to her?

42. Define the difference between Commitment and Involvement.

43. Are there degrees of commitment? Why or why not?

44. How would you apply Proverbs 15:1-2 to a married couple who argue about insignificant issues?

45. List, if you can, five things that were new to you that you learned from this study.

A Few Suggested Resources

Rather than a typical bibliography, I think it is more useful for the readers who wish to do further research to have some suggested resources. Though these are few, they give a student a good place to start.

Disclaimer: I am not necessarily endorsing these books. I am only listing them for possible continued research should the reader be interested.

Adams, Jay. *Marriage, Divorce, and Remarriage in the Bible.* Zondervan, 1986.

Duty, Guy. *Divorce & Remarriage: A Christian View.* Bethany House Publishers, 2002.

Eldredge, Robert Sr. *Can Divorced Christians Remarry?* Choice Publications, 2002.

House, H. Wayne (Editor), *Divorce and Remarriage: Four Christian Views.* InterVarsity Press, 1990.

Instone-Brewer, David. *Divorce and Remarriage in the Bible: The Social and Literary Context.* Wm. B. Eerdmans Publishing Company, 2002.

Keener, Craig S. *And Marries Another: Divorce and Remarriage in the Teaching of the New Testament.* Hendrickson Publishers, 1991.

Walston, Rick L "Josh." *Divorce and remarriage: An amplification of the Assemblies of God position paper on divorce and remarriage.* Gospel Publishing House, 1991.

White, James R. and Niell, Jeffrey D. *The Same Sex Controversy: Defending and Clarifying the Bible's Message About Homosexuality.* Bethany House Publishers, 2002.

About the Author

Dr. Walston and his wife, Sue, live in the Pacific Northwest. He served as a pastor and counselor in the Assemblies of God and independent churches for 20 years. Later he entered into the ministries of Christian education and writing. He is the president of Columbia Evangelical Seminary where he also serves as a professor. Columbia is a distance-learning school offering degrees through mentorship studies. For information see www.ColumbiaSeminary.edu.

Dr. Walston's educational background is extensive and includes a *Doctor of Ministry* from Bakke Graduate University, and a *Doctor of Philosophy* in New Testament Theology from North-West University. At the time of this writing, he is the author of four other books:

The Speaking in Tongues Controversy: The Initial, Physical Evidence of the Baptism in the Holy Spirit Debate (Wipf and Stock Publishers, 2005, ISBN: 1-59752-165-5. 236 pages).

Unraveling the Mystery of the Motivational Gifts: Your Gifts Discovery Manual (Wipf and Stock Publishers, 2005, ISBN: 1-59752-164-7. 238 pages).

Walston's Guide to Christian Distance Learning: Earning Degrees Nontraditionally, 4th Edition (Persuasion Press, 1999, ISBN: 0-973435-0-X, 176 pages).

Divorce and remarriage: An amplification of the Assemblies of God position paper on divorce and remarriage (Gospel Publishing House, 1991, 92 pages).

You can reach Rick Walston at:

Columbia Evangelical Seminary
Dr. Rick Walston, President
P. O. Box 1189
Buckley, WA 98321

or by e-mail at CES@tx3.net